I0455528

17th Amendment... Rescind!!!

by

Daniel H. Marchi

authorHOUSE®

AuthorHouse™
1663 Liberty Drive, Suite 200
Bloomington, IN 47403
www.authorhouse.com
Phone: 1-800-839-8640

©2008 Daniel H. Marchi. All rights reserved.

No part of this book may be reproduced, stored in a retrieval system, or transmitted by any means without the written permission of the author.

First published by AuthorHouse   10/6/2008

ISBN: 978-1-4389-1731-3 (sc)

Printed in the United States of America
Bloomington, Indiana

This book is printed on acid-free paper.

FRAMERS OF THE CONSTITUTION

Twelve (12) sovereignty, States Governments' delegates whom wrote the Constitution that creates a Republic form of Government (Legislative Executive and Judiciary) are known today as Framers of the Constitution.

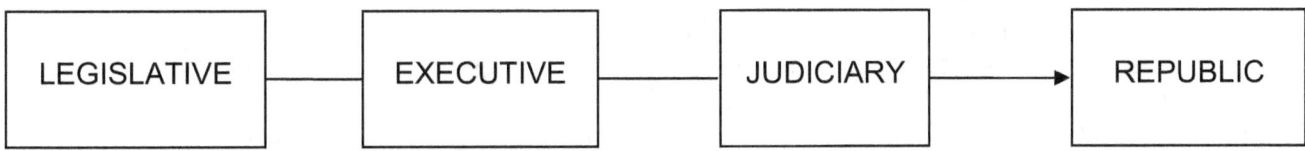

The Legislative branch is made up with United States Senate and the House of Representatives.

With most interest of States Governments' delegates whom are States Governments' Ambassadors to be called Senators in mind, the United States Senate was made to be the representative body of States' Governments.

The United States Senate (Ambassadors) is the most important position in the Federal Government being given the authority of the most active component of the legislative Federal Government's branch.

The most important group of members are in the States Governments' Legislatures. A States Government's Legislature is made up of State Senate and State Assembly members whom the State's inhabitance elected into office; therefore, the State's people indirectly participate in the Federal Government's decision-making through the States Governments' Legislatures.

The Framers of the Constitution authorized the States Governments' Legislatures to choose two senators (ambassadors). The tenure of these two United States senators (ambassadors) would be six (6) years. The States Governments' Legislatures are given the power to remove senators during the senator's tenure. Since election are to be in sequence every two (2) years, one third(1/3) of the United States' senators (ambassadors) would be up for election at anyone time. Two thirds (2/3) of the United States' senators (ambassadors) would be in office maintaining stability of the Federal Government during elections. At the end of a single senator's tenure, all senators of the Federal Government would have gone through elections.

In reverse, tearing up the Constitution would eliminate the Federal Government (United States Senate, The House of Representatives and the position of President of the United States). The States' Governments within the United States territory would reduce to it's original form of being independent, Sovereign, States' Governments of a Democratic form of Government.

In conclusion, the Framers of the Constitution made the United States Senate the ambassadors of States' Governments through the elected choice of the States Governments' Legislatures whom would protect the rights of the States Governments' inhabitances guaranteeing the sovereignty of States' Governments within a Republic.

In Supreme Court explaining its decision, the majority of members observed that States' Governments through proportional representation in the United States Senate (ambassadors) retain sufficient influence over the federal political process to insure their autonomy and sovereign interests.

PROPORTIONAL REPRESENTATION

The Framers of the Constitution came to a great compromise at the Constitutional Convention of 1787. They provided for proportional and quasi equal representation for the House of Representatives and the United States Senate through the states within the United State's territory. Proportion Representation means that a sovereign state's area is subdivided into representative regions of equal or quasi equal population. The symbol for Proportion Representation in this paper is ◯

Not Proportion Representation means a person represents the entire population of the United States, state or state's district. The symbol for Not Proportion Representation in this paper is ⬡

- The Supreme Court does not have to protect the States Governments' sovereignties.
- The Constitution Balances the nature of mortal men against other mortal men's desires for power as watchdogs against each others encroachment of power with the States' Governments through the United States Senate (ambassadors) watching the Federal Government.
- The horizontal separation of powers divides the power to govern into three branches the executive, the legislative, and the judicial leaving no one department of government with enough power to abuse the people within the territory of the United States.
- The Framers of the Constitution smoothed out power between the States' Governments through the United States Senate (ambassadors) and Federal Government.
- States Governments' sovereignties result in decentralizing Federal Government power.
- Campaign financing is eliminated for United States Senates' (ambassadors) seats.
- The United States Senate (ambassadors) duties plays an important part in the bicameral (United States Senate (ambassadors) and House of Representatives) system of government.
- Power is divided between the Federal Government and the States Governments Legislatures through the United States Senate (ambassadors).
- The Federal Government is granted limited powers requiring cooperation of the States' Governments through the United States Senate (ambassadors) in the area of national defense, foreign affairs, and interstate commerce.
- The remaining power is left to the States' Governments and it's people eliminating the Federal Government's ability to abuse the constituencies of the States' Governments.
- The Framers of the Constitution gave the States' Governments through the United States Senate (ambassadors) the responsibility of governing the people of the Republic.

BICAMERALISM

Bicameralism brought together two independent power sources. The people's representatives in the United States House of representatives and the state legislatures' agents in the United States Senate; therefore, the need for two powers to concur would, in turn, thwart the influence of special interests groups.

The Framers of the constitution borrowed bicameralism from the British system of government dividing the legislative branch into two chambers (United States Senate (ambassadors) and House of Representatives). The upper bicameral chamber is the United States Senate (ambassadors) whose members represent quasi equal contingencies' districts and the lower bicameral chamber is the House of Representatives whose members also represent quasi equal contingencies' districts

The United States Senate (ambassadors) is an essential element of federalism (the political doctrine of the former Federalist Party) which included bicameralism (United States Senate (ambassadors) and House of Representatives).

Bicameralism (United States Senate (ambassadors) and House of Representatives) thwarts corporate lobbyist and other special interest groups safeguarding the interests of the States' Governments and the constituencies within States' Governments.

Bicameralism guarantees human rights of the individuals and suppresses corporate lobbyist and other special interest groups that might take those human rights away.

Bicameralism (United States Senate (ambassadors) and House of Representatives) is preserved in a Republic.

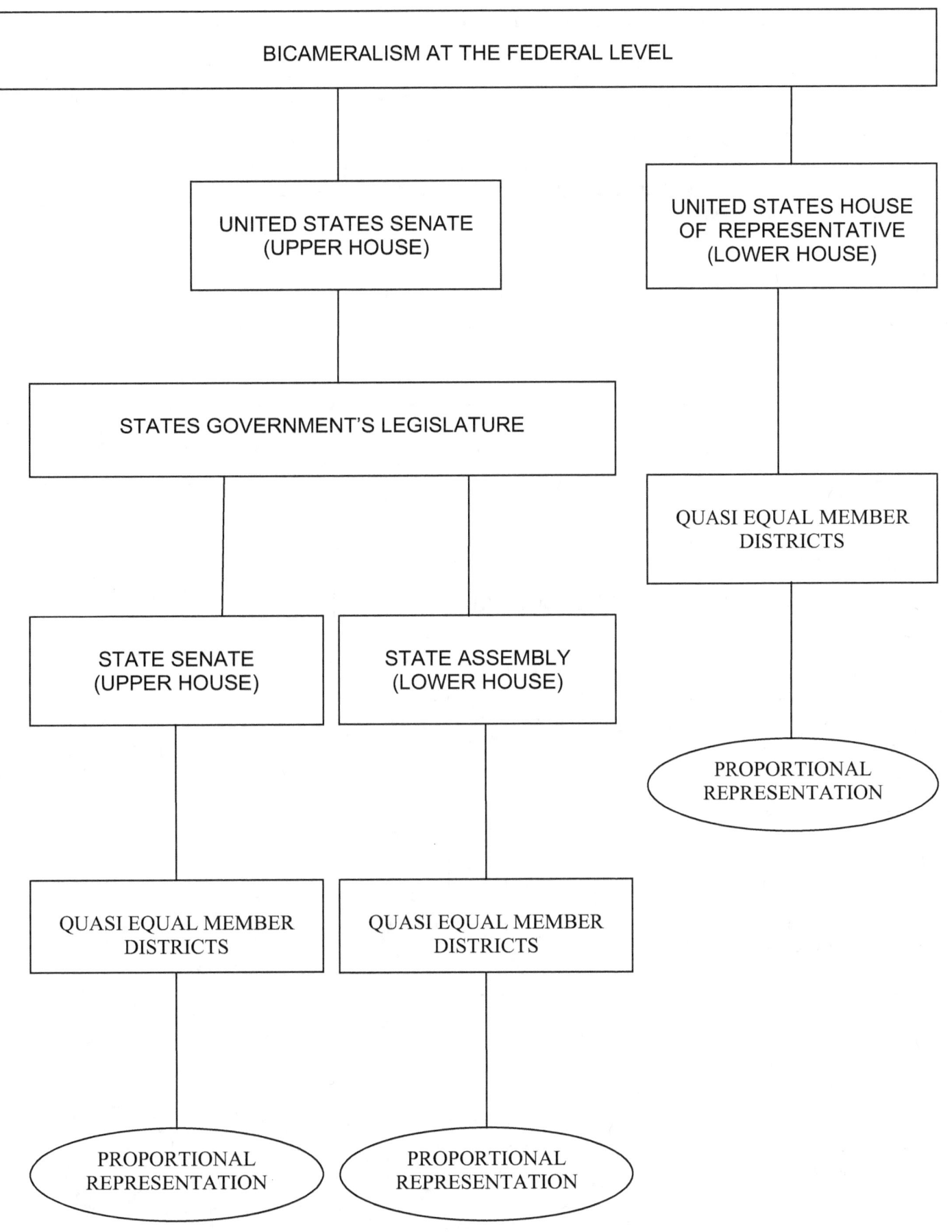

BICAMERALISM AT THE FEDERAL LEVEL

UNITED STATES SENATE
(UPPER HOUSE)

UNITED STATES HOUSE
OF REPRESENTATIVE
(LOWER HOUSE)

STATES GOVERNMENT'S LEGISLATURE

QUASI EQUAL MEMBER
DISTRICTS

STATE SENATE
(UPPER HOUSE)

STATE ASSEMBLY
(LOWER HOUSE)

PROPORTIONAL
REPRESENTATION

QUASI EQUAL MEMBER
DISTRICTS

QUASI EQUAL MEMBER
DISTRICTS

PROPORTIONAL
REPRESENTATION

PROPORTIONAL
REPRESENTATION

DESCRIBING QUASI EQUAL MEMBER DISTRICTS AND PROPORTIONAL REPRESENTATION
LEGISLATIVE BRANCH

The Framers of the Constitution provided for proportional representation in the United States House of Representatives and proportional representation for the States Governments' Legislatures whom chose the members of United States Senate.

State Senate, State Assembly and House of Representatives must represent quasi equal member districts to meet the criteria for proportional representation. Since the States Governments' Legislatures is made of the State Senate and Assembly, the States Governments' Legislatures would be proportional representation.

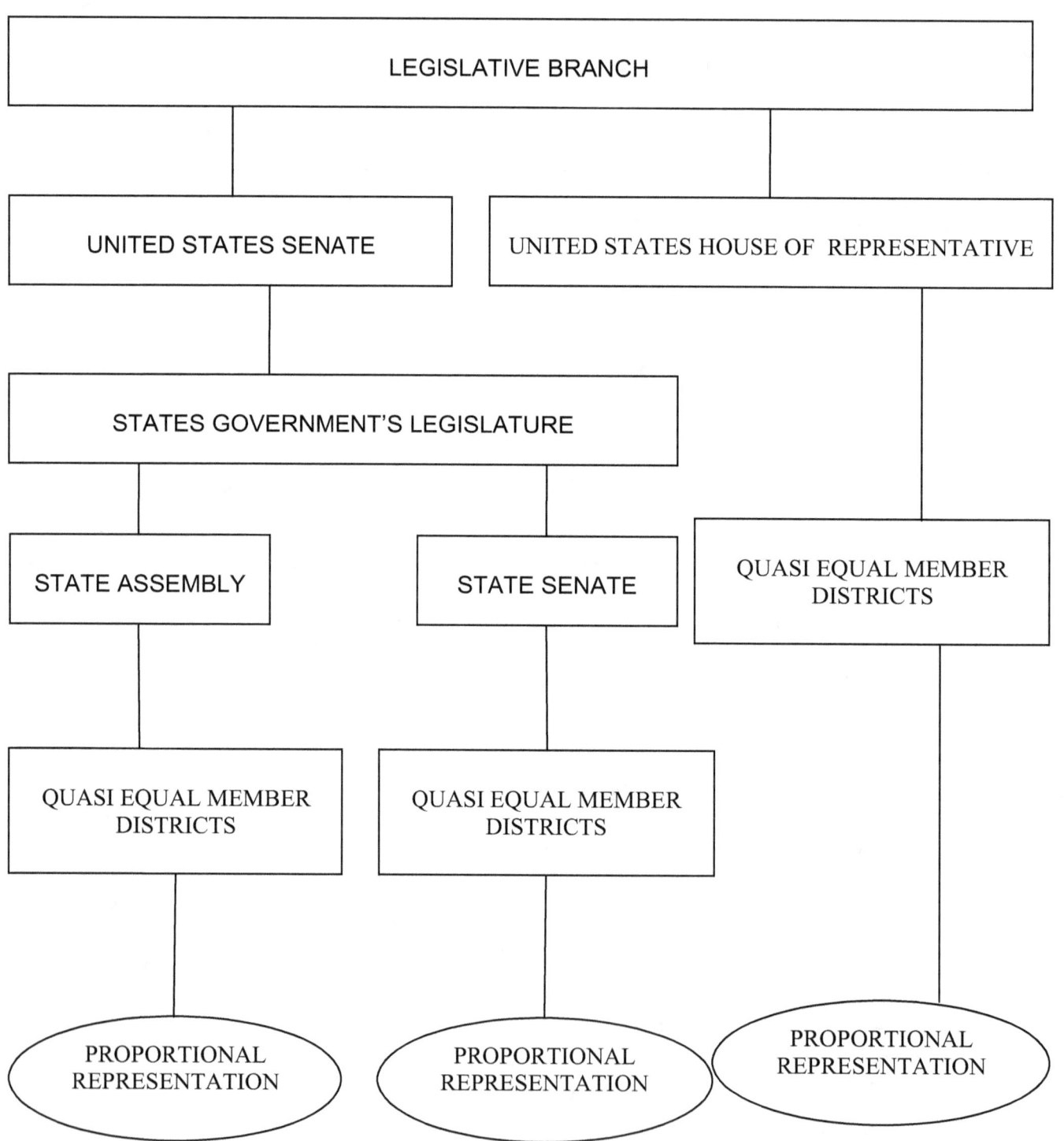

STATES' GOVERNMENTS (PROPORTIONAL REPRESENTATION)

The population of the entire state votes for States' Governors; therefore the quasi equal members' districts do not exist. The States' Governors fall in the realm of being non proportional representation indicating that dictatorial powers exists.

The States Governments' Legislatures consist of proportional representation State's Senates and proportional representation State's Assemblies; therefore, States Governments' Legislatures are proportional representation.

The States' Governors deal with proportional representation States Governments' Legislatures; therefore, the States' Governors fall in the realm of being proportional representation

The States' Governments are made up of the States' Governors and States Governments' Legislatures; therefore, States' Governments are proportional representation.

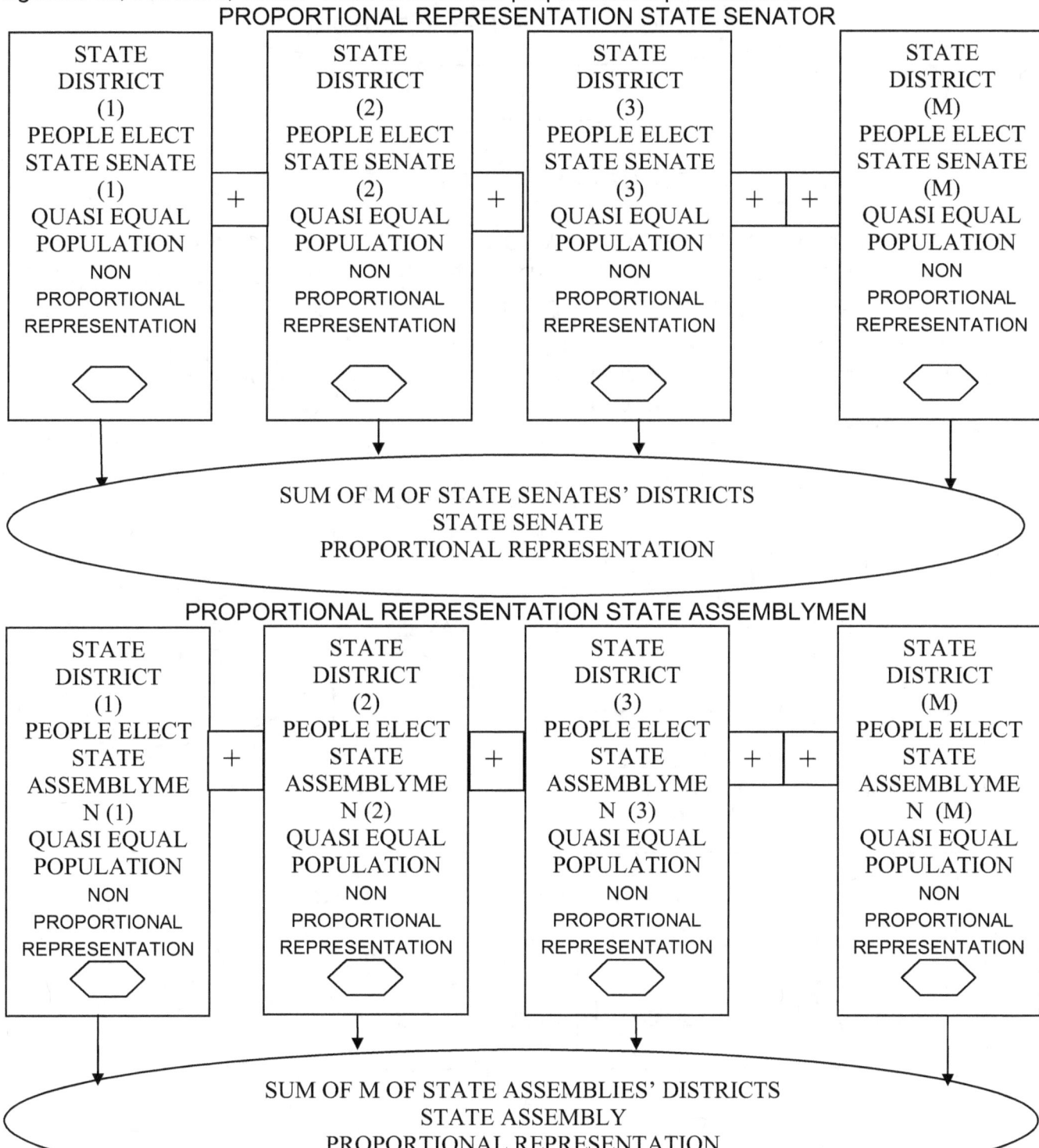

PROPORTIONAL REPRESENTATION OF A STATE LEGISLATURE

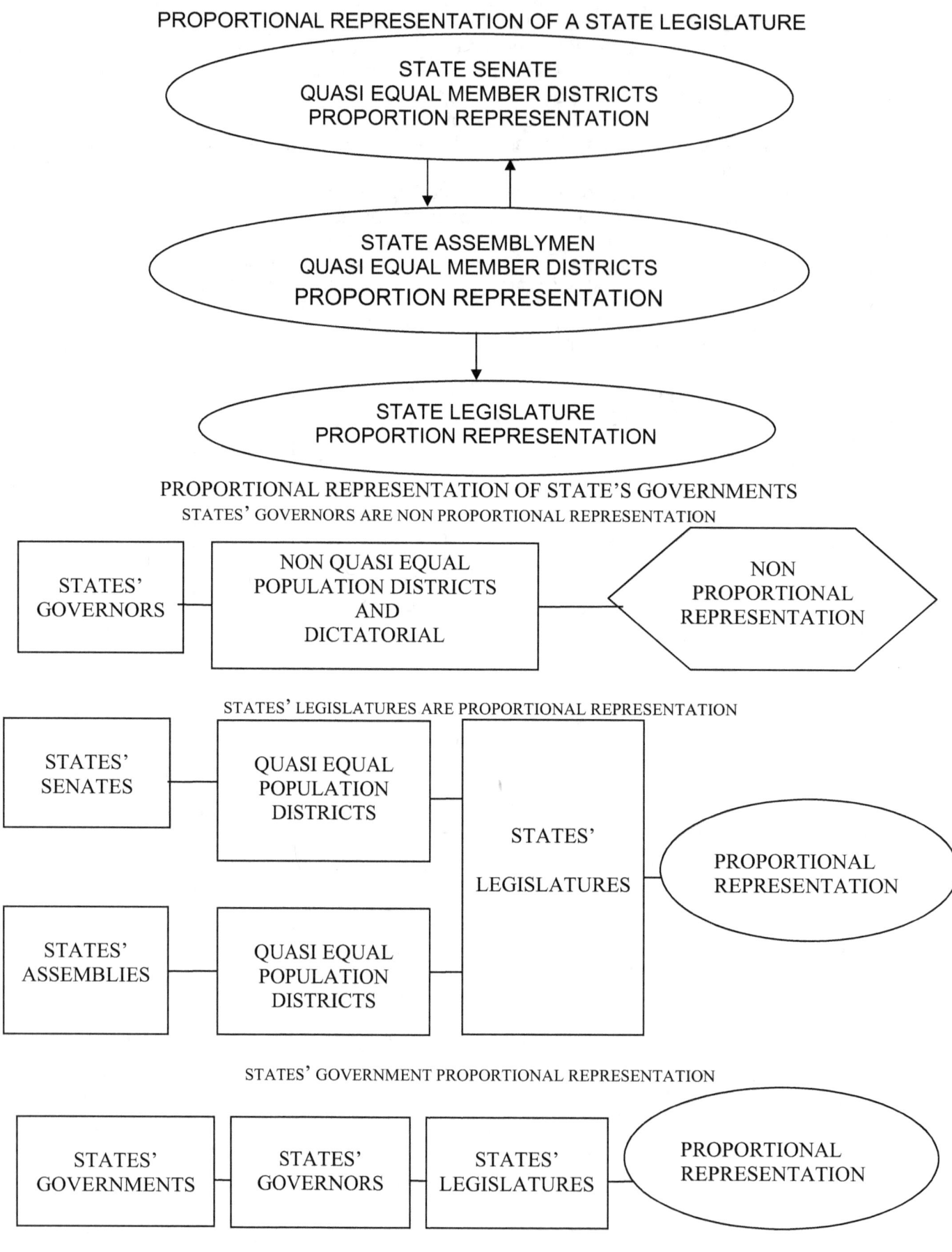

STATE SENATE
QUASI EQUAL MEMBER DISTRICTS
PROPORTION REPRESENTATION

STATE ASSEMBLYMEN
QUASI EQUAL MEMBER DISTRICTS
PROPORTION REPRESENTATION

STATE LEGISLATURE
PROPORTION REPRESENTATION

PROPORTIONAL REPRESENTATION OF STATE'S GOVERNMENTS

STATES' GOVERNORS ARE NON PROPORTIONAL REPRESENTATION

STATES' GOVERNORS — NON QUASI EQUAL POPULATION DISTRICTS AND DICTATORIAL — NON PROPORTIONAL REPRESENTATION

STATES' LEGISLATURES ARE PROPORTIONAL REPRESENTATION

STATES' SENATES — QUASI EQUAL POPULATION DISTRICTS — STATES' LEGISLATURES — PROPORTIONAL REPRESENTATION

STATES' ASSEMBLIES — QUASI EQUAL POPULATION DISTRICTS

STATES' GOVERNMENT PROPORTIONAL REPRESENTATION

STATES' GOVERNMENTS — STATES' GOVERNORS — STATES' LEGISLATURES — PROPORTIONAL REPRESENTATION

FEDERAL GOVERNMENT (PROPORTIONAL REPRESENTATION)

Since States Governments' are proportional representation the States' legislatures selects the members of the United States Senate (ambassadors) whom are to be considered as proportional representation.

The Federal Government is made up of United States Senate (ambassadors), House of Representatives and President of the United States. In reality, the Federal Government is made up of the States Governments' Legislatures , House of Representatives and President of the United States.

Since the electoral college picks whose members represent proportional representation States' Legislatures the President of the United States is proportional representation.

The Federal Government contains the proportional representation President of the United States, the proportional representation Senate (ambassadors) and the proportional representation United House of Representatives. The United States of America is a Republic.

The Framers of the Constitution authorized the States Governments' Legislatures to choose two senators (ambassadors). The tenure of these two United States senators (ambassadors) would be six (6) years. The States Governments' Legislatures are given the power to remove senators during the senator's tenure.

PROPORTIONAL REPRESENTATION UNITE STATES HOUSE OF REPRESENTATIVES

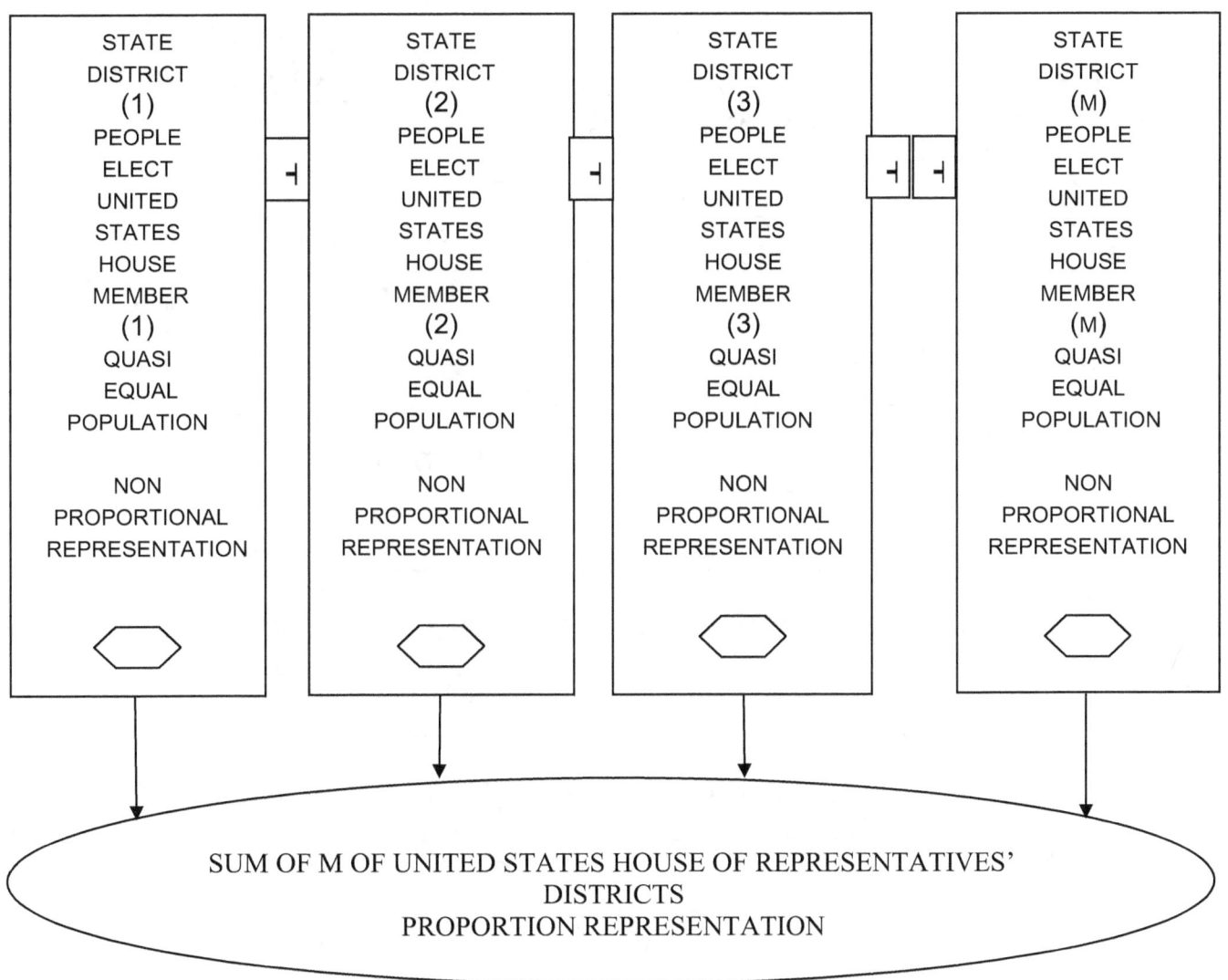

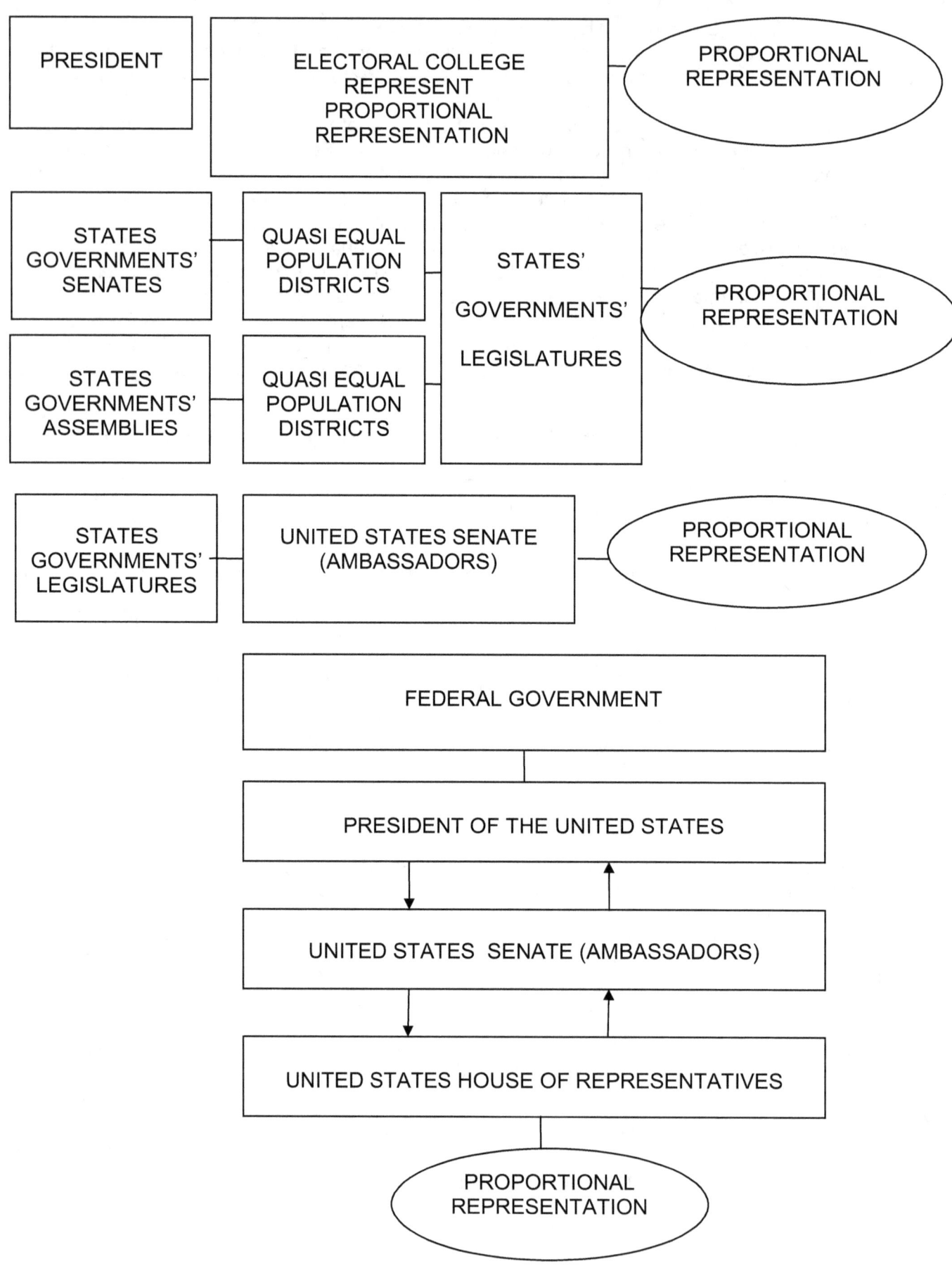

17TH AMENDMENT

Introducing in 1913 the 17th Amendment reduced the Republic to two separate independent governmental bodies - States' Governments and a Federal Government.

The authority of selecting United States senators as ambassadors of States' Governments was removed from the States Governments' Legislatures whom protected the rights of the States' Governments people.

The States' inhabitants lost their rights of participating in the Federal Government. The Republic of United States diminishes to the Democracy of the United States.

Protecting States Governments' sovereignties and the rights of the people within is left to the Tenth Amendment in the Bill of Rights and the Supreme Court.

The 17th Amendment requires that the people of a State's Government select two United States senators to the United States Federal Government relegating the United States Senate to be non proportional representation.

Since the electoral college picks whose members represent proportional representation States' Legislatures the President of the United States is proportional representation.

The Federal Government contains the proportional representation President, the United States non proportional representation Senate (people elected) and the proportional representation United House of Representatives. The United States of America is now a democracy.

The Federal Government is non proportional representation. The territory of the United States of America contains a Democratic form of Government.

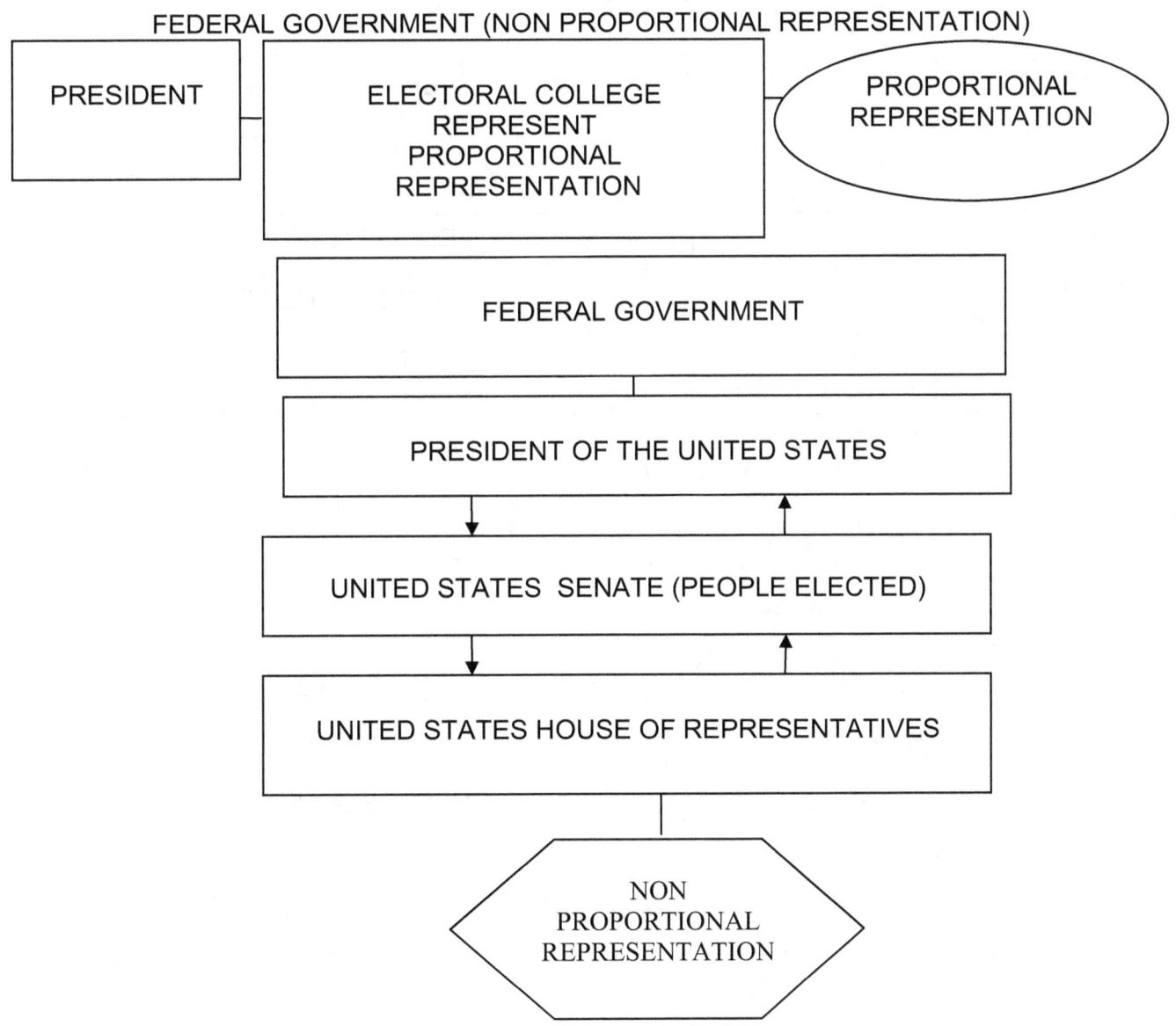

9

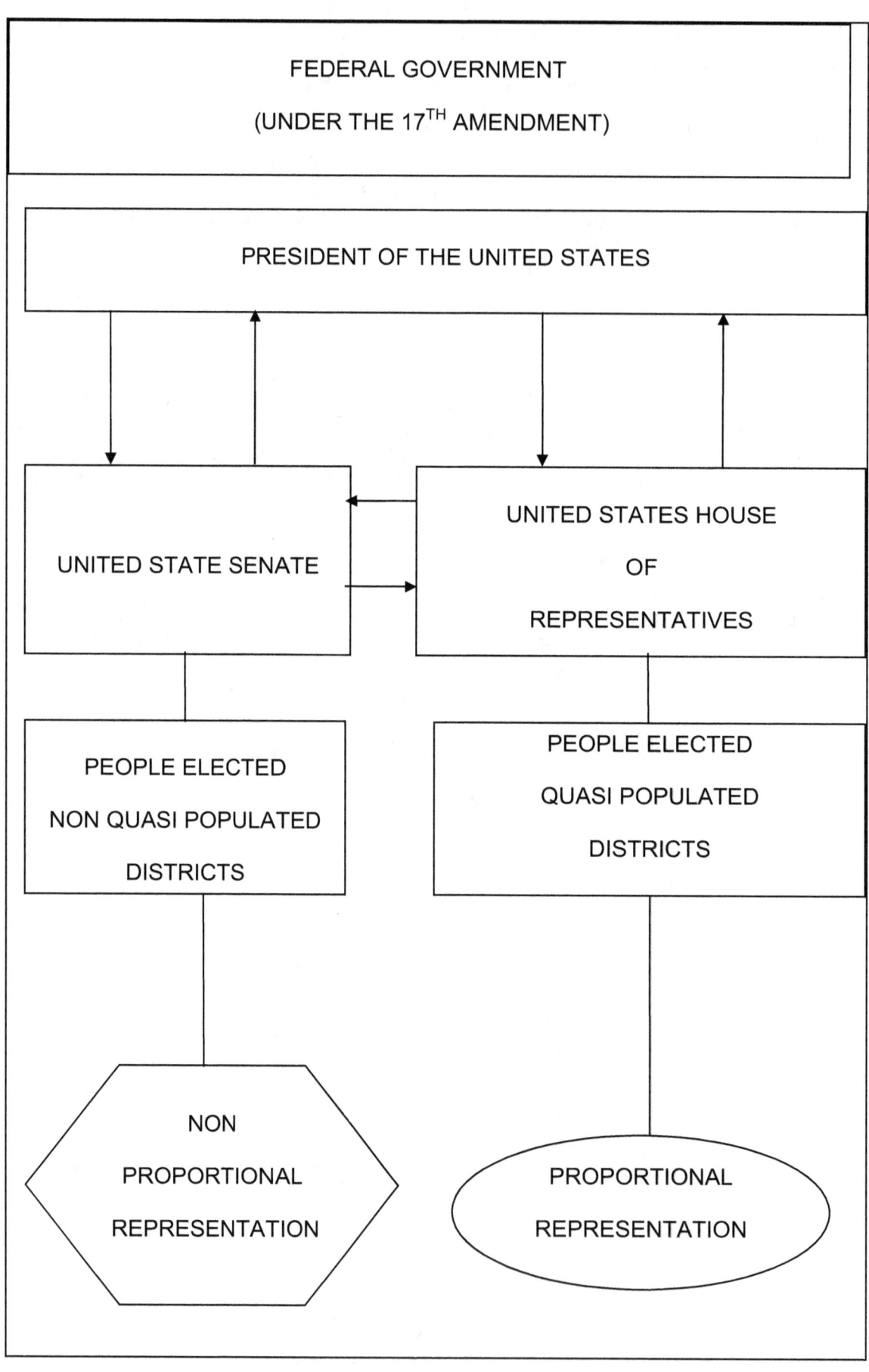

LOGROLLING

- The constituencies represented in the United States House of representatives and Senate (People elected) are the same facilitating creation of logrolling agreements across the two houses of the Federal Government making procurement of special interest legislation easier and allowing special interests to directly lobby the Senate (People elected) especially critical in interstate commerce where development of groups interests lies across state lines.
- Huge concentrations of business, capital, and labor introduces the senators to the elite. Alliances are created with corporations and special interests during senator elections.
- The United States Senate (People elected) is an independent political body with dictatorial powers. A group of senators (People elected) might dictate rather than legislate resulting in trying to gain control of the government.
- The Federal Government creates growth with grant programs due to United States Senate (People elected) participation.
- Tremendous power of the mass media on the senators (People elected) may influence their individual deliberations.
- The power is transferred to non elected and appointed Federal Government officials whom are not accountable to the constituencies of the States' Governments.
- Out of control, appointed official do not restore the lost accountability to the States' Governments and the States' Governments' constituencies taking away the States' sovereignties, peoples' sovereignties and rights.
- Senators might rely on popular opinion polls in determining the course of national policy.
- In an era of increasing interstate commerce there exists development groups across state lines whose procurement of special interest legislation is made easy especially through the United Sates Senate (People elected).
- Due to Senate (People elected) participation, intrusion of the Federal Government occurs. Typical examples are illegal immigration, extensive granting of visas and green cards satisfying the appetites of corporation to create a third world salary labor market.
- Senate (People elected) often threaten to filibuster proceedings.
- The policies of Senators (People elected) are leaning towards the ideals of Globalization pointing to a new world order.
- Senators' (People elected) "green card" programs created a surplus of unemployed American workers in the market place encouraging cheap labor practices..
- Senators' (People elected) "green card" programs created a double edge sword of third world wages in the United States and abroad.
- Senators' (People elected) "green card" programs is the product of elite corporate lobbyist who are only interested in cheap labor.
- Senators (People elected) don't confer with States Governments Legislatures to stop the tide of illegal aliens.
- Senators (People elected) want amnesty for illegal aliens.

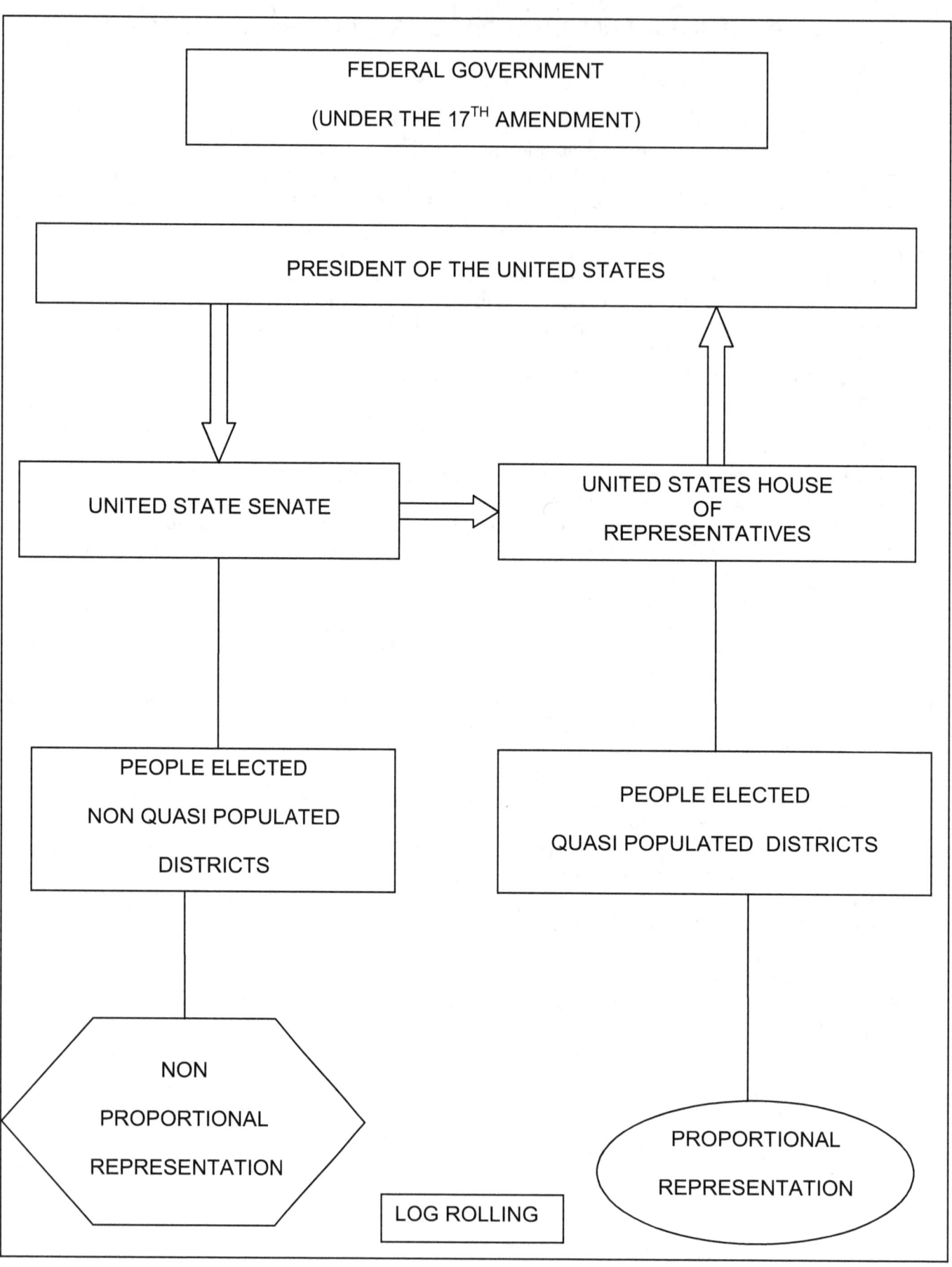

FEDERAL GOVERNMENT

(UNDER THE 17TH AMENDMENT)

PRESIDENT OF THE UNITED STATES

UNITED STATE SENATE

UNITED STATES HOUSE OF REPRESENTATIVES

PEOPLE ELECTED

NON QUASI POPULATED

DISTRICTS

PEOPLE ELECTED

QUASI POPULATED DISTRICTS

NON

PROPORTIONAL

REPRESENTATION

LOG ROLLING

PROPORTIONAL

REPRESENTATION

UNITED STATES HOUSE OF REPRESENTATIVES COURT OF LAST RESULTS

- Sometimes House of Representative takes the place of the void States Governments Legislatures to protect the rights of the citizenry within the United States territory.
- The House of Representative dead locked the President and Senate (People elected) into excepting the "illegal aliens" House of Representative's bill.
- The House of Representative dead locked the President and Senate (People elected) amnesty for illegal aliens and guest work programs.
- The House of Representative dead locked the President and Senate (People elected) into excepting border security and enforcement measure.
- The House of Representative is the trigger that stops the Senate (People elected) and Presidents ideal of Globalization pointing to a new world order for cheap wages..

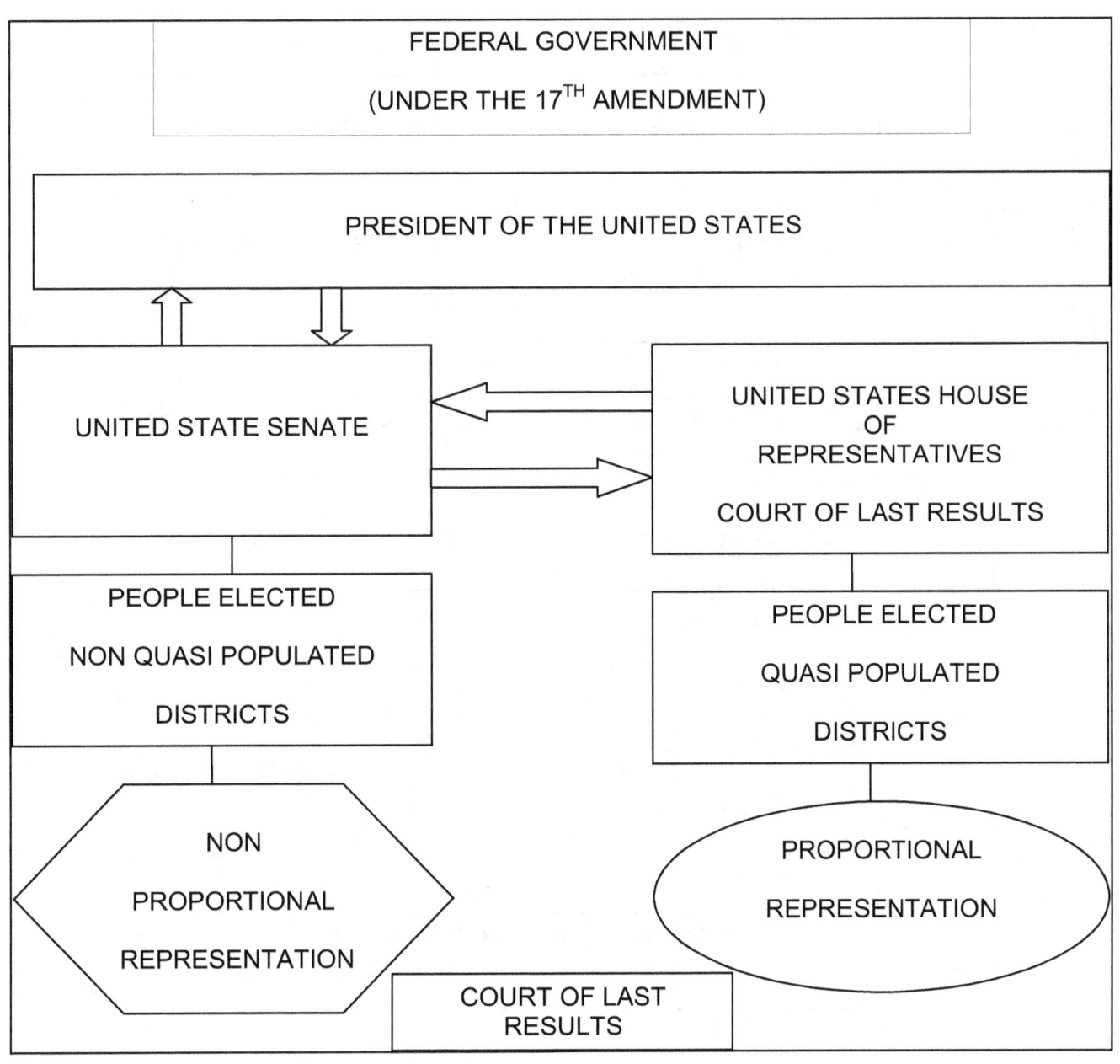

STALEMATE PRESIDENTIAL APPOINTMENTS

- Senate (People elected) often threaten to filibuster President appointments.
- Senate (People elected) often threaten to impeach the President.
- Senate (People elected) often threaten to remove Presidential appointees.

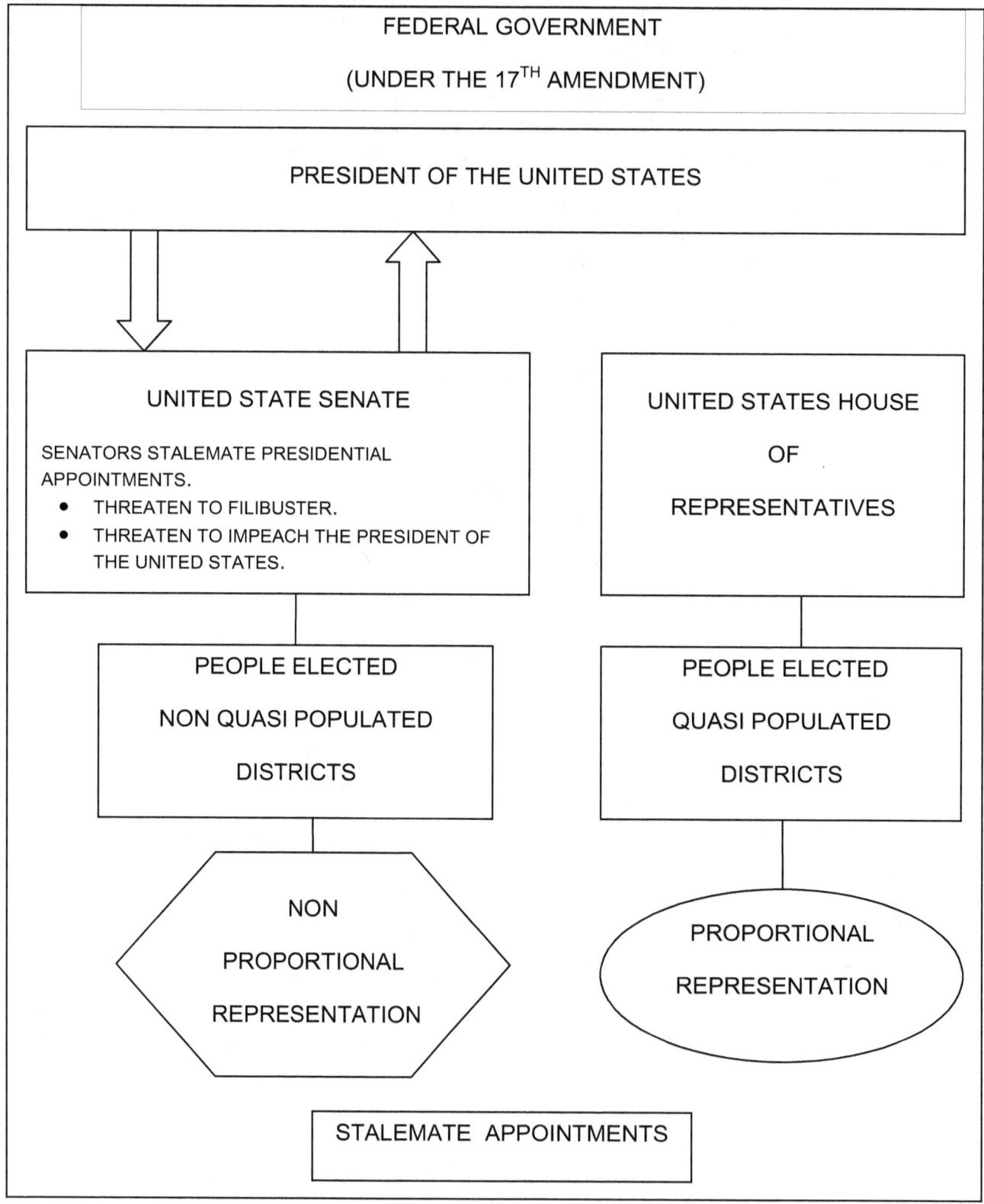

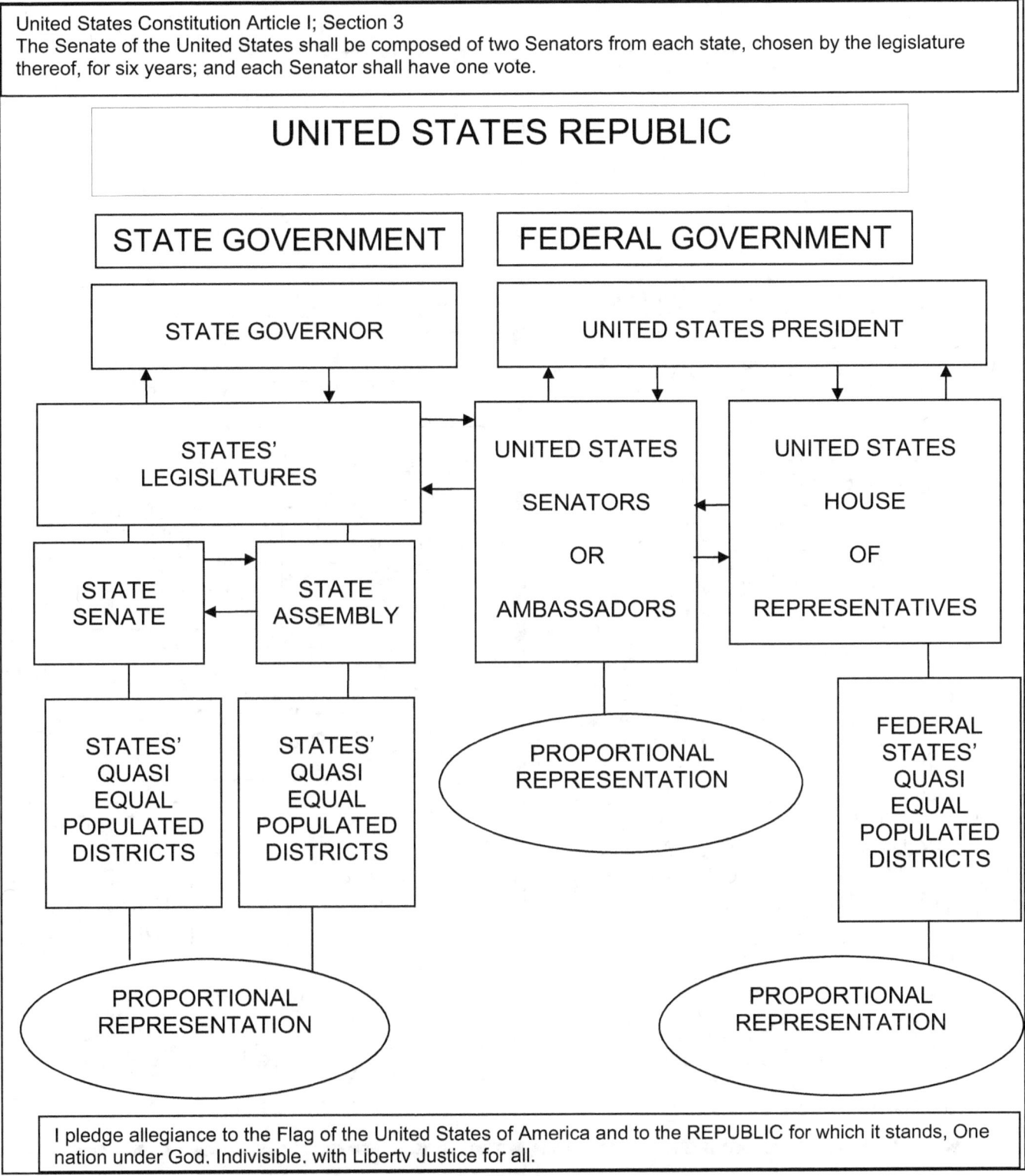

United States Constitution Article I; Section 3
The Senate of the United States shall be composed of two Senators from each state, chosen by the legislature thereof, for six years; and each Senator shall have one vote.

UNITED STATES REPUBLIC

STATE GOVERNMENT

FEDERAL GOVERNMENT

STATE GOVERNOR

UNITED STATES PRESIDENT

STATES' LEGISLATURES

UNITED STATES SENATORS OR AMBASSADORS

UNITED STATES HOUSE OF REPRESENTATIVES

STATE SENATE

STATE ASSEMBLY

STATES' QUASI EQUAL POPULATED DISTRICTS

STATES' QUASI EQUAL POPULATED DISTRICTS

PROPORTIONAL REPRESENTATION

FEDERAL STATES' QUASI EQUAL POPULATED DISTRICTS

PROPORTIONAL REPRESENTATION

PROPORTIONAL REPRESENTATION

I pledge allegiance to the Flag of the United States of America and to the REPUBLIC for which it stands, One nation under God. Indivisible. with Libertv Justice for all.

Fig. 1

In Fig. 1, the commentary of the flow chart the word Senators could be replaced with the word ambassadors. The State Legislators decide on the appointment of the two Senators to represent state interest in the Federal Government. Proportion Representation is ensured (proven later).

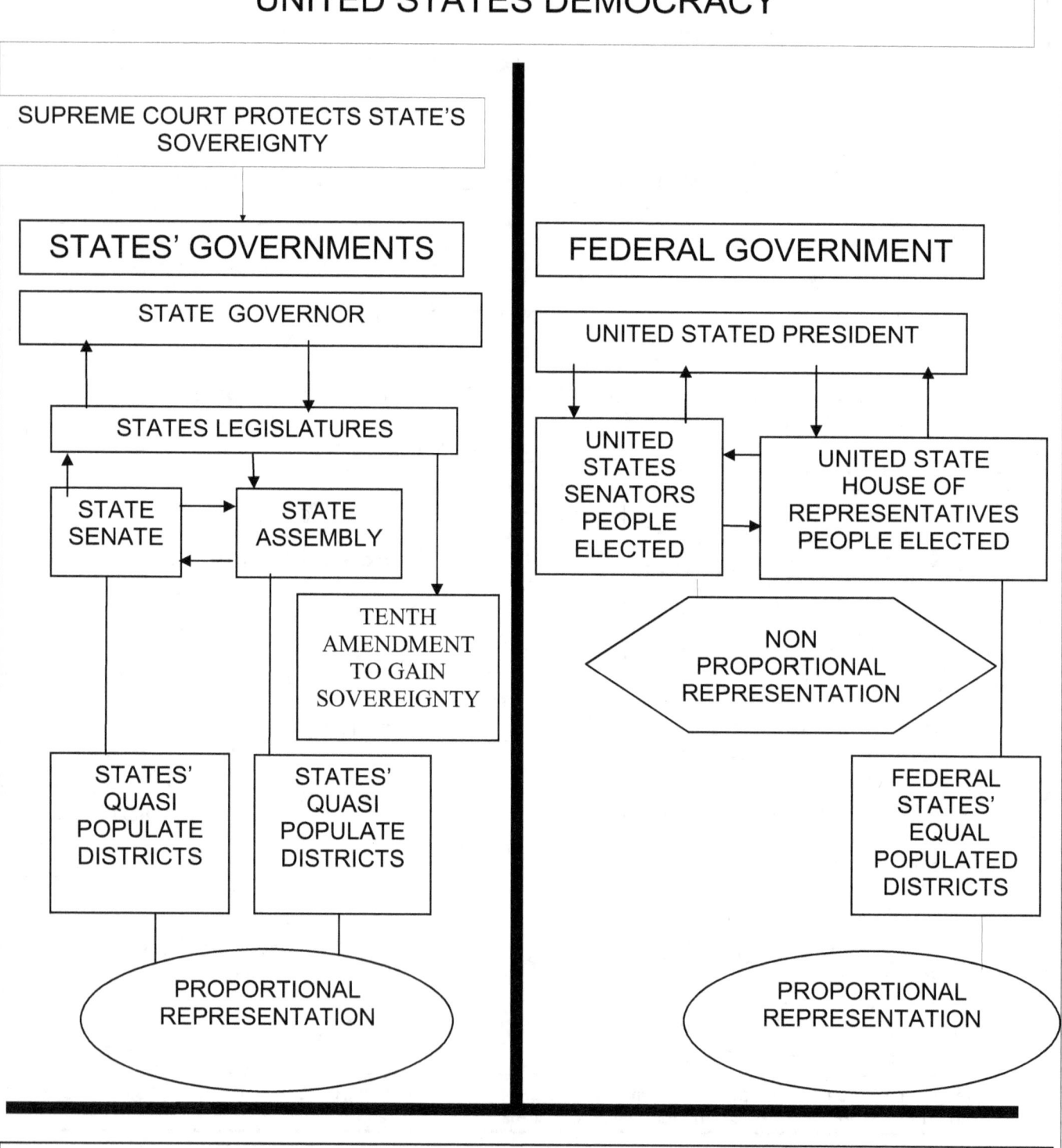

United States Constitution Seventeenth Amendment Clause 1. The Senate of the United States shall be composed of two Senators from each State, elected by the people thereof, for six years; and each Senator shall have one vote

UNITED STATES DEMOCRACY

SUPREME COURT PROTECTS STATE'S SOVEREIGNTY

STATES' GOVERNMENTS

FEDERAL GOVERNMENT

STATE GOVERNOR

UNITED STATED PRESIDENT

STATES LEGISLATURES

STATE SENATE

STATE ASSEMBLY

UNITED STATES SENATORS PEOPLE ELECTED

UNITED STATE HOUSE OF REPRESENTATIVES PEOPLE ELECTED

TENTH AMENDMENT TO GAIN SOVEREIGNTY

NON PROPORTIONAL REPRESENTATION

STATES' QUASI POPULATE DISTRICTS

STATES' QUASI POPULATE DISTRICTS

FEDERAL STATES' EQUAL POPULATED DISTRICTS

PROPORTIONAL REPRESENTATION

PROPORTIONAL REPRESENTATION

I pledge allegiance to the Flag of the United States of America and to the DEMOCRACIES for which it stands, One nation under God, Indivisible, with Liberty Justice for all.

Fig. 2

The break as indicated in the flow chart of Fig. 2 shows that there now exists two systems of governments. One is a State System and the other is a Federal system. Both State System and Federal system represent the people of the presuming sovereign states of the United State of America under the 17th Amendment.

In the commentary of the flow chart the word Senators could be replaced with the two words Federal Governors since both the State Governors' and United States Senators' constituents are within the same states' boundaries.

Going back to Fig. 2, Amendment 17th promoted Ambassadors to Federal Governors who are not committed to anyone for the six years of their tenure. When the Constitution was being written, the Framers of the Constitution did not have this setup in mind

The state of West Virginia is used as an example of a Proportion Representation accomplishment.

CONSTITUTION OF WEST VIRGINIA

ARTICLE VI

6-1. The Legislature.

The legislative power shall be vested in a Senate and House of Delegates. The style of their acts shall be, "Be it enacted by the Legislature of West Virginia."

6-2. Composition of Senate and House of Delegates.

The Senate shall be composed of twenty-four, and the House of Delegates of sixty-five members, subject to be increased according to the provisions hereinafter contained.

6-4. Division of state into Senatorial districts.

For the election of Senators, the state shall be divided into twelve senatorial districts, which number shall not be diminished, but may be increased as hereinafter provided. Every district shall elect two Senators, but, where the district is composed of more than one county, both shall not be chosen from the same county. The districts shall be compact, formed of contiguous territory, bounded by county lines, and, as nearly as practicable, equal in population, to be ascertained by the census of the United States. After every such census, the Legislature shall alter the senatorial districts, so far as may be necessary to make them conform to the foregoing provision.

6-6. Provision for delegate representation.

For the election of delegates, every county containing a population of less than three fifths of the ratio of representation for the House of Delegates, shall, at each apportionment, be attached to some contiguous county or counties, to form a delegate district.

The executive department shall consist of a governor.

7-2. Election. An election for governor at such times and places as may be prescribed by law.

The following algorithm will succeed to guarantee the Proportion Representation of the House of representatives.

The membership of the United States House of Representatives changes each decade following the decennial United States Census. Each state is apportioned a number of Congressional members based upon the state's population. For N member of people in the Congressional House of Representatives, compute

$$A = P/\sqrt{n/(n+1)}$$

for 50 American states where P is the population constant of the state being evaluated and n is the latest state's number of seats, there will always exist A and n values for each state.

Cycle=1. The algorithm begins letting n=1 and compute A for each P's population for all 50 states.

Cycle=2. From the 50 list of A numbers pick the largest A value relating to a state and increase the n value of that state by 1 and recalculate a new A value for that state.

Cycle=3. From the 50 list of A numbers pick the largest A value relating to a state and increase the n value of that state by 1 and recalculate a new A value for that state.

Cycle=N. From the 50 list of A numbers pick the largest A value relating to a state and increase the n value of that state by 1 and recalculate a new A value for that state.

Each state creates districts of approximately equal population

$$Z = P/n$$

where Z is a whole number and the number of persons in a district.

Computing P'= Z x n. P will not equal P' in many cases. The state, in creating the district size must take this situation into account. In other words,

$$P=P' + \text{epsilon}$$

The value of epsilon is the number of persons left over. The number epsilon might be small compared to the number of persons in the district; therefore, epsilon can be ignored using the theory of large numbers.

Increasing the value of N, will increase the number of House of Representative members resulting in reducing district sizes.

CONSTITUTION OF WEST VIRGINIA

ARTICLE 1

Representatives to Congress.

For the election of representatives to Congress, the state shall be divided into districts, corresponding in number with the representatives to which it may be entitled; which districts shall be formed of contiguous counties, and be compact. Each district shall contain, as nearly as may be, an equal number of population (quasi equal), to be determined according to the rule prescribed in the constitution of the United States. Proportion Representation is accomplished.　　　○

FLOW CHARTS AND TABLES 17TH AMENDMENT

Prior to the ratification of the 17 Amendment, the States Governments' Legislatures elected and sent ambassadors to the United States Senate. The United States Senate (Ambassadors) and United States House of Representatives became two independent powers resulting in a bicameral legislative branch of government having quasi equal districts.

After the ratification of 17th Amendment, States Governments' inhabitances elected the United States senators. The upper house United States Senate (People elected) does not have quasi equal districts; therefore, the United States Senate (People elected) and the United States House of Representatives (People Elected) become two dependent powers eliminating the bicameral legislative branch of government resulting in changing a Republic form of Government to a centralized Democratic form of government where the authority of the legislative branch sometimes tries to dominate the executive branch.

Keeping the people elected legislative branch modes of election the same constituencies, the two powers, United States Senate (people elected) and the United States House of Representatives (people elected), can not in most cases thwart the influence of special interests groups upon the centralized Federal Government. Also, the peoples Federal Government's rights don't exists and the United States senators' domains become super United States House of Representatives members' domains. Furthermore, the United States senators (People elected) do not always zealously go over board to protecting the Federal Government people's rights and the States Governments sovereignties.

Within the legislative branch, since the United States House of Representative reflects the views of the people within the States Governments' boundaries in a quasi equal districts manner, the United States Senate (People elected) most likely will choose to discuss Federal Governments' affairs with large corporations instead of with the States Governments' Legislatures whom know the desires of the people. The United States Senate (People elected) is more powerful than the United States House of Representatives (People elected) in terms of their responsibilities making the United States Senate (People elected) vulnerable to lobbyist of elite corporations whose only aim is to lower wages and possibly take control of the United States government.

For example, Enron and other corporations financed United States senators (People elected) campaigns, amounting to millions of dollars. As a result, those United States senators will often discuss impending legislation with these corporations on a routine bases before discussing impending legislation with States Governments Legislatures or with the people who elected those United States senators into office.

Finally, the communication between the States Governments Legislatures and the Federal Government (United States Senate (People elected), United States House of Representatives and the President) does not exists; and, therefore, the checks and balances has been eliminated among the three branches of government with the Judicious branch and Tenth Amendment protecting the sovereignties of the States' Governments and the Federal Government rights of the States Governments' inhabitances.

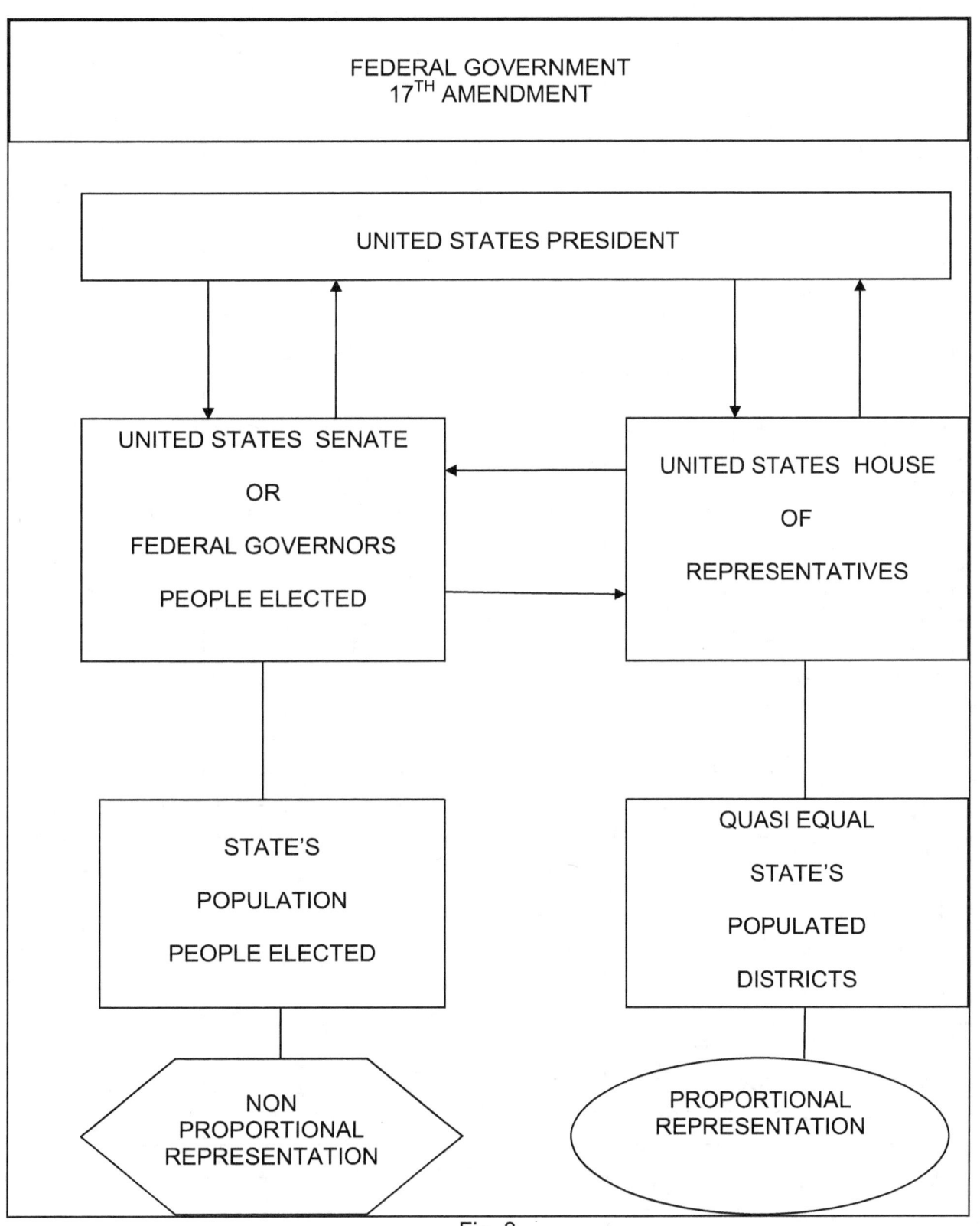

Fig. 3

State	A Population	B USA Senators or Federal Governors	C USA House members	D People elect within a USA Senators Or Federal Governors district	E People elect within a USA House district
Alabama	4,500,752	1	7	4,500,752	642,965
Alaska	648,818	1	1	648,818	648,818
Arizona	5,580,811	1	8	5,580,811	697,601
Arkansas	2,725,714	1	4	2,725,714	681,429
California	35,484,453	1	53	35,484,453	669,518
Colorado	4,550,688	1	7	4,550,688	650,098
Connecticut	3,483,372	1	5	3,483,372	696,674
Delaware	817,491	1	1	817,491	817,491
Florida	17,019,068	1	25	17,019,068	680,763
Georgia	8,684,715	1	13	8,684,715	668,055
Hawaii	1,257,608	1	2	1,257,608	628,804
Idaho	1,366,332	1	2	1,366,332	683,166
Illinois	12,653,544	1	19	12,653,544	665,976
Indiana	6,195,643	1	9	6,195,643	688,405
Iowa	2,944,062	1	5	2,944,062	588,812
Kansas	2,723,507	1	4	2,723,507	680,877
Kentucky	4,117,827	1	6	4,117,827	686,305
Louisiana	4,496,334	1	7	4,496,334	642,333
Maine	1,305,728	1	2	1,305,728	652,864
Maryland	5,508,909	1	8	5,508,909	688,614
Massachusetts	6,433,422	1	10	6,433,422	643,342
Michigan	10,079,985	1	15	10,079,985	671,999
Minnesota	5,059,375	1	8	5,059,375	632,422
Mississippi	2,881,281	1	4	2,881,281	720,320
Missouri	5,704,484	1	9	5,704,484	633,832
Montana	917,621	1	1	917,621	917,621
Nebraska	1,739,291	1	3	1,739,291	579,764
Nevada	2,241,154	1	3	2,241,154	747,051
New Hampshire	1,287,687	1	2	1,287,687	643,844
New Jersey	8,638,396	1	13	8,638,396	664,492
New Mexico	1,874,614	1	3	1,874,614	624,871
New York	19,190,115	1	29	19,190,115	661,728
North Carolina	8,407,248	1	13	8,407,248	646,711
North Dakota	633,837	1	1	633,837	633,837
Ohio	11,435,798	1	18	11,435,798	635,322
Oklahoma	3,511,532	1	5	3,511,532	702,306
Oregon	3,559,596	1	5	3,559,596	711,919
Pennsylvania	12,365,455	1	19	12,365,455	650,813
Rhode Island	1,076,164	1	2	1,076,164	538,082
South Carolina	4,147,152	1	6	4,147,152	691,192

	A	B	C	D	E
State	Population	USA Senators or Federal Governors	USA House members	People elect within a USA Senators Or Federal Governors district	People elect within a USA House district
South Dakota	764,309	1	1	764,309	764,309
Tennessee	5,841,748	1	9	5,841,748	649,083
Texas	22,118,509	1	32	22,118,509	691,203
Utah	2,351,467	1	3	2,351,467	783,822
Vermont	619,107	1	1	619,107	619,107
Virginia	7,386,330	1	11	7,386,330	671,485
Washington	6,131,445	1	9	6,131,445	681,272
West Virginia	1,810,354	1	3	1,810,354	603,451
Wisconsin	501,242	1	8	501,242	62,655
Wyoming	501,242	1	1	501,242	501,242
TOTAL	285,275,336	50	435	285,275,336	32,838,666

Table A

Table A is used to compare number of United States Senators (People elected) against number of United States House of Representative members. Since the people of the entire state elect the Senators, a one is placed in column B; whereas, the federal government uses an algorithm to calculate the number of the House of Representative's members for each state based upon the state's population.

.Comparing columns' D and E, one House of Representative's member in column E has less or equal number people to represent ; whereas, one United States Senators (People elected) in column D represents all the people in the state like a Governor.
For each State Government,

1 Senator (Federal Governor)<=(less than or equal to) Representative members

Where

100=Senators(Federal Governors)<(less than) 435=House of Representative members

As shown in the inequality expression, the Senators are actually Federal Governors with no one restraining them but the House of Representatives.

The House of Representative is another Federal body. Furthermore, at present, the President only deals with the United States Senate (People elected) and the House of Representative.
Later on, solid facts will be presented to show that States' Governments dominate the Federal Government within their boundaries demanding that States' Governments must be players in the President's decision making.

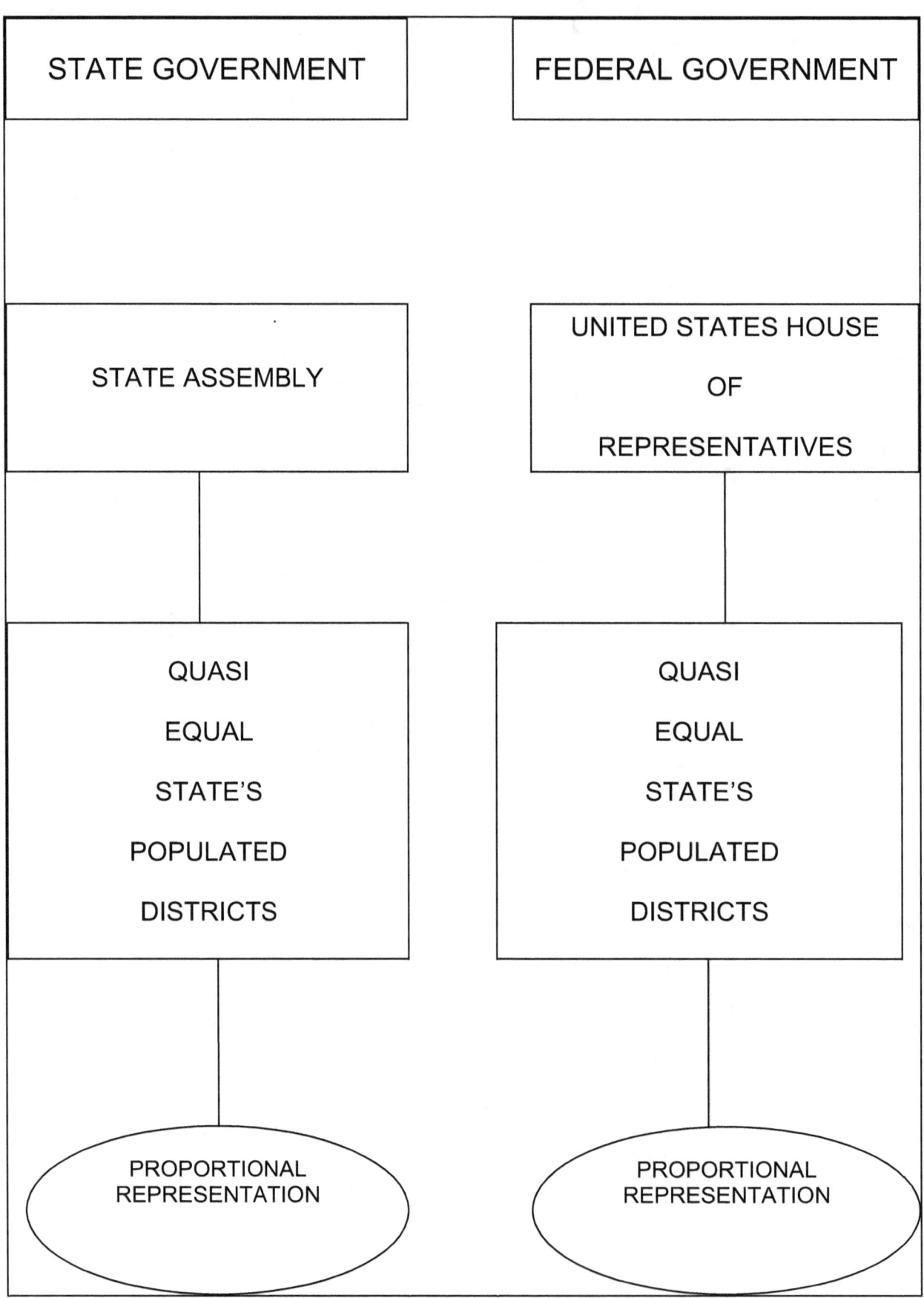

Fig. 4

State	A Population	B State Assembly members	C USA House members	D People elect Members within a State's Assembly district	E People elect within a USA House district
Alabama	4,500,752	105	7	42,864	642,965
Alaska	648,818	40	1	16,220	648,818
Arizona	5,580,811	60	8	93,014	697,601
Arkansas	2,725,714	100	4	27,257	681,429
California	35,484,453	80	53	443,556	669,518
Colorado	4,550,688	65	7	70,011	650,098
Connecticut	3,483,372	120	5	29,028	696,674
Delaware	817,491	35	1	23,357	817,491
Florida	17,019,068	120	25	141,826	680,763
Georgia	8,684,715	180	13	48,248	668,055
Hawaii	1,257,608	50	2	25,152	628,804
Idaho	1,366,332	70	2	19,519	683,166
Illinois	12,653,544	118	19	107,233	665,976
Indiana	6,195,643	100	9	61,956	688,405
Iowa	2,944,062	100	5	29,441	588,812
Kansas	2,723,507	126	4	21,615	680,877
Kentucky	4,117,827	100	6	41,178	686,305
Louisiana	4,496,334	105	7	42,822	642,333
Maine	1,305,728	151	2	8,647	652,864
Maryland	5,508,909	65	8	84,752	688,614
Massachusetts	6,433,422	40	10	160,836	643,342
Michigan	10,079,985	110	15	91,636	671,999
Minnesota	5,059,375	67	8	75,513	632,422
Mississippi	2,881,281	122	4	23,617	720,320
Missouri	5,704,484	163	9	34,997	633,832
Montana	917,621	100	1	9,176	917,621
Nebraska	1,739,291	49	3	35,496	579,764
Nevada	2,241,154	41	3	54,662	747,051
New Hampshire	1,287,687	400	2	32,192	643,844
New Jersey	8,638,396	80	13	107,980	664,492
New Mexico	1,874,614	42	3	44,634	624,871
New York	19,190,115	150	29	127,934	661,728
North Carolina	8,407,248	120	13	70,060	646,711
North Dakota	633,837	94	1	6,743	633,837
Ohio	11,435,798	99	18	115,513	635,322
Oklahoma	3,511,532	101	5	34,768	702,306
Oregon	3,559,596	60	5	59,327	711,919
Pennsylvania	12,365,455	203	19	60,914	650,813
Rhode Island	1,076,164	75	2	14,349	538,082
South Carolina	4,147,152	124	6	33,445	691,192
South Dakota	764,309	70	1	10,919	764,309
Tennessee	5,841,748	98	9	59,610	649,083
Texas	22,118,509	150	32	147,457	691,203
Utah	2,351,467	75	3	31,353	783,822
Vermont	619,107	148	1	4,183	619,107
Virginia	7,386,330	99	11	74,609	671,485
Washington	6,131,445	49	9	125,132	681,272
West Virginia	1,810,354	65	3	27,852	603,451

	A	B	C	D	E
State	Population	State Assembly members	USA House members	People elect Members within a State's Assembly district	People elect within a USA House district
Wisconsin	501,242	98	8	5,115	62,655
Wyoming	501,242	60	1	8,354	501,242
TOTAL	285,275,336	4435	435	3,066,071	32,838,666

Table B

Table B compares the State Assembly numbers against the House of Representative numbers. The number of State Assembly members is higher than the number of House of Representative members. The State Assembly members communicate with less people than the House of Representative; therefore, at the state's level, the State Government dominates the Federal Government. The greater the disparity in the numbers the more dominance the State Assembly members have over the House of Representative.

State	USA House Members	<	State Senate Members	<	State Assembly Members
Alabama	7	<	35	<	105
Alaska	1	<	20	<	40
Arizona	8	<	30	<	60
Arkansas	4	<	35	<	100
California	53	<	40	<	80
Colorado	7	<	35	<	65
Connecticut	5	<	30	<	120
Delaware	1	<	21	<	35
Florida	25	<	40	<	120
Georgia	13	<	56	<	180
Hawaii	2	<	20	<	50
Idaho	2	<	35	<	70
Illinois	19	<	59	<	118
Indiana	9	<	50	<	100
Iowa	5	<	50	<	100
Kansas	4	<	40	<	126
Kentucky	6	<	38	<	100
Louisiana	7	<	39	<	105
Maine	2	<	35	<	151
Maryland	8	<	47	<	65
Massachusetts	10	<	40		
Michigan	15	<	38	<	110
Minnesota	8	<	67		
Mississippi	4	<	50	<	122
Missouri	9	<	34	<	163
Montana	1	<	50	<	100
Nebraska	3	<	49	<	49
Nevada	3	<	21	<	41
New Hampshire	2	<	24	<	400
New Jersey	13	<	40	<	80
New Mexico	3	<	42		
New York	29	<	62	<	150
North Carolina	13	<	50	<	120
North Dakota	1	<	47	<	94
Ohio	18	<	33	<	99
Oklahoma	5	<	48	<	101
Oregon	5	<	30	<	60

State	USA House Members	<	State Senate Members	<	State Assembly Members
Pennsylvania	19	<	50	<	203
Rhode Island	2	<	38	<	75
South Carolina	6	<	46	<	124
South Dakota	1	<	35	<	70
Tennessee	9	<	33	<	98
Texas	32	<	31	<	150
Utah	3	<	29	<	75
Vermont	1	<	14	<	148
Virginia	11	<	40	<	99
Washington	9	<	49		
West Virginia	3	<	24	<	65
Wisconsin	8	<	33	<	98
Wyoming	1	<	30	<	60
TOTAL	435	<	1,932	<	4,682

Table B'

At all times in the future, the Governors and Legislatures must design their districts to surpass the Federal number of House of Representative members.

Since the Federal Government has to make arrangement for fifty states in the union, a cap is imposed on the total number of House of Representative number. Limits on the number of House of representatives is a constraint that the Federal Government must adhere to for practical reasons. This acts to the advantage of the States' Governments.

The degree of dominance over the Federal Government at the States' Governments level are directly proportion to number of State Assembly member's numbers exceeding the House of Representative member numbers.

The State Government becomes a formal opponent to the Federal Government to fight for the rights of the state

As illustrated in Table B in pairs of columns B-C and D-E, the States' Governments or Legislatures currently attunes to the feeling of their people within their sovereign boundaries more than the Federal government does. Table B' is a simple representation of Table B in inequality form.

Keep in mind that the number of districts assigned to the States' Governments Senate must also be greater than the House of Representatives to ensure the dominance that the State Senate has over the House of Representative. The important fact is that both the States' Governments Senate and the States Governments' Assemblies make up the Legislatures whom deal with the States' Governors in decision making. The outcome of any resolution to a debate within the States' Legislatures pertaining to subjects within the states governments boundaries would be much more accurate than the Federal government. The relationship among the number of members in the inequality expression is

House of Representative<(less than) State Senate<(less than) State assembly   (1)

The more the differences the greater the States' Governments dominate the Federal government putting the state in a demanding situation instead of a lobbying one.

States' Governments presently relinquishes their sovereign powers to the Federal Government to a pathetic state of having to lobby for favors in stead of demanding them.

This situation must be reversed for the future of our Republic. The supremacy of States' Governments over the Federal Government within its sovereign boundaries demands that. power belongs to the State Government within its sovereign borders as depicted in Table B COLUMNS B-C AND D-E. This is the most important fact!

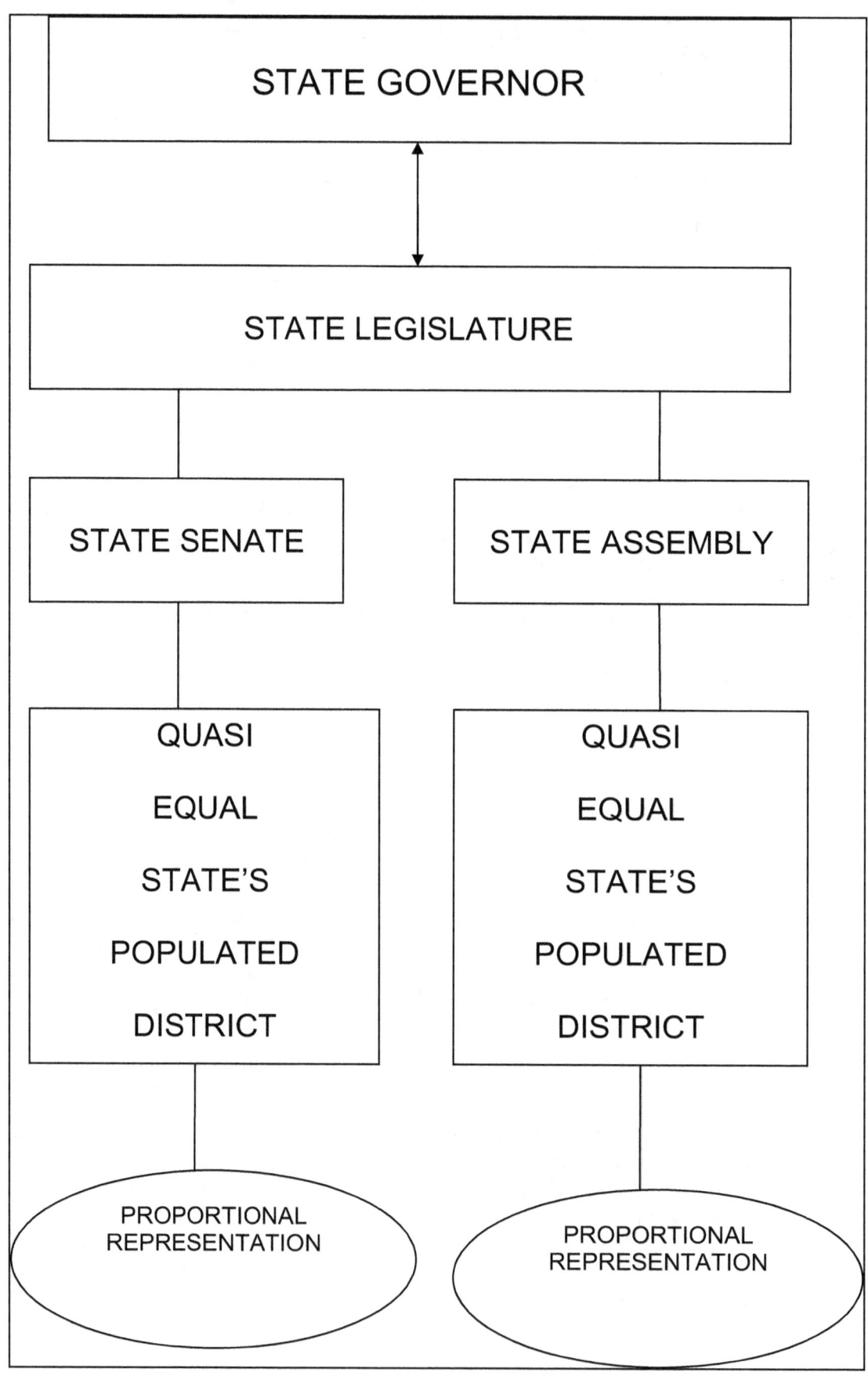

Fig. 5

	A	C	B	E	D
State	Population	State Senators members	State Assembly members	People within a State Senator's district	People within a State Assembly's district
Alabama	4500752	35	105	128,593	42,864
Alaska	648818	20	40	32,441	16,220
Arizona	5580811	30	60	186,027	93,014
Arkansas	2725714	35	100	77,878	27,257
California	35484453	40	80	887,111	443,556
Colorado	4550688	35	65	130,020	70,011
Connecticut	3483372	30	120	116,112	29,028
Delaware	817491	21	35	38,928	23,357
Florida	17019068	40	120	425,477	141,826
Georgia	8684715	56	180	155,084	48,248
Hawaii	1257608	20	50	62,880	25,152
Idaho	1366332	35	70	39,038	19,519
Illinois	12653544	59	118	214,467	107,233
Indiana	6195643	50	100	123,913	61,956
Iowa	2944062	50	100	58,881	29,441
Kansas	2723507	40	126	68,088	21,615
Kentucky	4117827	38	100	108,364	41,178
Louisiana	4496334	39	105	115,291	42,822
Maine	1305728	35	151	37,307	8,647
Maryland	5508909	47	65	117,211	84,752
Massachusetts	6433422	40		160,836	
Michigan	10079985	38	110	265,263	91,636
Minnesota	5059375	67		75,513	
Mississippi	2881281	50	122	57,626	23,617
Missouri	5704484	34	163	167,779	34,997
Montana	917621	50	100	18,352	9,176
Nebraska	1739291	49		35,496	
Nevada	2241154	21	41	106,722	54,662
New Hampshire	1287687	24	400	53,654	32,192
New Jersey	8638396	40	80	215,960	107,980
New Mexico	1874614	42	42	44,634	44,634
New York	19190115	62	150	309,518	127,934
North Carolina	8407248	50	120	168,145	70,060
North Dakota	633837	47	94	13,486	6,743
Ohio	11435798	33	99	346,539	115,513
Oklahoma	3511532	48	101	73,157	34,768
Oregon	3559596	30	60	118,653	59,327
Pennsylvania	12365455	50	203	247,309	60,914
Rhode Island	1076164	38	75	28,320	14,349
South Carolina	4147152	46	124	90,155	33,445
South Dakota	764309	35	70	21,837	10,919

State	A Population	C State Senators members	B State Assembly members	E People within a State Senator's district	D People within a State Assembly's district
Tennessee	5841748	33	98	177,023	59,610
Texas	22118509	31	150	713,500	147,457
Utah	2351467	29	75	81,085	31,353
Vermont	619107	14	148	44,222	4,183
Virginia	7386330	40	99	184,658	74,609
Washington	6131445	49	49	125,132	125,132
West Virginia	1810354	24	65	75,431	27,852
Wisconsin	501242	33	98	15,189	5,115
Wyoming	501242	30	60	16,708	8,354
TOTAL	285,275,336	1932	4435	7,175,011	2,794,226

Table C

The States Governments' Senate dominates the States Governments' Assemblies in that the States Governments' Senators serve a longer term in office. Since the States Governments Senators' numbers are lower than the States Governments Assemblies' numbers, the States Governments Senators' districts overshadows the States Governments Assemblies' districts.

Like the Federal Senators the State Senators' election are staggered keeping a percentage of them off the election circuit.

Remember that the members of House of Representative, States Governments' Senate and States Governments' Assemblies are PROPORTIONAL REPRESENTATION.

When the States Governments' legislatures choose a United States Senator to represent the State Government, the United States Senator becomes an ambassador whose aim is to represent the objectives of the state as a whole not the random ideals of the state's people who are not attune to the their States Governments' intentions within the Federal Government.

When the President deals with the United States' Senators (Ambassadors), he will be dealing with the ideas of States' Governments and not those of egocentric United States Senators (People elected) installed under the 17th Amendment which put them in the category of NON PROPORTIONAL REPRESENTATION.

State	A State Senate	B State Assembly	C USA House	D USA House 2x Colum C	E USA House 3x Colum C
Alabama	35	105	7	14	21
Alaska	20	40	1	3	4
Arizona	30	60	8	16	24
Arkansas	35	100	4	9	13
California	40	80	53	99	152
Colorado	35	65	7	14	20
Connecticut	30	120	5	11	16
Delaware	21	35	1	3	5
Florida	40	120	25	47	72
Georgia	56	180	13	25	30
Hawaii	20	50	2	5	6
Idaho	35	70	2	5	7
Illinois	59	118	19	37	57
Indiana	50	100	9	19	28
Iowa	50	100	5	10	14
Kansas	40	126	4	9	13
Kentucky	38	100	6	13	19

State	A State Senate	B State Assembly	C USA House	D USA House 2x Colum C	E USA House 3x Colum C
Louisiana	39	105	7	14	21
Maine	35	151	2	5	7
Maryland	47	65	8	16	25
Massachusetts	40		10	19	29
Michigan	38	110	15	30	45
Minnesota	67		8	15	23
Mississippi	50	122	4	9	14
Missouri	34	163	9	17	26
Montana	50	100	1	4	5
Nebraska	49	49	3	6	9
Nevada	21	41	3	7	10
New Hampshire	24	400	2	5	7
New Jersey	40	80	13	25	39
New Mexico	42		3	6	9
New York	62	150	29	56	86
North Carolina	50	120	13	24	37
North Dakota	47	94	1	3	4
Ohio	33	99	18	34	52
Oklahoma	48	101	5	11	16
Oregon	30	60	5	11	16
Pennsylvania	50	203	19	37	56
Rhode Island	38	75	2	4	6
South Carolina	46	124	6	13	19
South Dakota	35	70	1	3	4
Tennessee	33	98	9	18	26
Texas	31	150	32	62	94
Utah	29	75	3	8	11
Vermont	14	148	1	3	4
Virginia	40	99	11	22	33
Washington	49		9	18	27
West Virginia	24	65	3	6	9
Wisconsin	33	98	8	17	25
Wyoming	30	60	1	3	3
TOTAL	1,932	4,682	435	870 2x435	1305 3x435

Table D

Table D is an expansion table that describes the power of today's States Governments' Legislatures. The federal Government sets today's number of House of Representatives for the entire United States at 435.

A program had to be written containing an algorithm to calculated the expansion in columns D and E of the new numbers of United States Representatives for each state based on the state's population.

Looking at the total's row of Table D, the number 435 has been expanded to two and three times to produce the corresponding number of House of Representatives. Comparing these new numbers in columns D and E of House of Representatives to the original State Senate and Assembly ones in column A and B, the State Senate and Assembly (Legislator) numbers dominate. Notice the nationwide numbers in the total row level of columns D and E.

A few comments are in order.

California needs more members in both State Senate and State Assembly.

Florida membership is weak!

Massachusetts does not have a State Assembly and State Senate membership is weak!

Ohio needs more members in both State Senate and State Assembly.

Pennsylvania could use more State Senators.

Virginia the State Senate finally peters out.

Washington does not have a State Assembly

Even with these mentioned deficiencies the state governments prevails in contacting people within their borders over the Federal government as is seen in Table D.

A constraint is that the Federal Government must adhere to a cap on the number of House of Representatives. The Framers of the Constitution set up two Senators (Ambassadors) for each state. One hundred Senators (Ambassadors) would complete the Federal Government's system that would be in total contact with the people of the United States of America.

Insuring the dominance of State Government over the Federal Government within their borders, remember to always apply the inequality expression (1).

DEFINITIONS

PRESIDENT OF THE UNITED STATES

Since the electors of the states within the whole country picks the President of the United States, the President falls within the realm of PROPORTIONAL REPRESENTATION.

STATE GOVERNOR

Since the whole state votes for the State Governor, the Governor falls within realm of NON PROPORTIONAL REPRESENTATION

A SENATOR (FEDERAL GOVERNOR) UNDER THE 17TH AMENDMENT

Since the whole state population votes for a Senator (Federal Governor), a Senator falls within the realm of NON PROPORTIONAL REPRESENTATION.

THE SENATE (FEDERAL GOVERNORS) UNDER THE 17TH AMENDMENT (ALL MEMBERS)

Since the population of the states within the United States varies considerably, the Senate also falls within the realm of NON PROPORTIONAL REPRESENTATION.

A HOUSE OF REPRESENTATIVE MEMBER

Since the district's population votes for a House of Representative member, the House of Representative district falls within the realm of NON PROPORTIONAL REPRESENTATION.

HOUSE OF REPRESENTATIVE (ALL MEMBERS)

Since members' districts have quasi equal population within the United States , the House of Representatives falls within the realm of PROPORTIONAL REPRESENTATION.

INDIVIDUAL STATE SENATOR MEMBER

Since the district's population votes for a State Senator, the State Senator's district falls within the realm of NON PROPORTIONAL REPRESENTATION.

STATE SENATE (ALL MEMBERS)

Since members' districts have quasi equal populations within the state's sovereign boundary, the State Senate falls within the realm of PROPORTIONAL REPRESENTATION.

INDIVIDUAL STATE ASSEMBLY MEMBER

Since the district's population votes for a State Assembly member, the State Assembly member's district falls within the realm of NON PROPORTIONAL REPRESENTATION.

STATE ASSEMBLY (ALL MEMBERS)

Since all members' districts have quasi equal population, within the state's sovereign boundary, the State Assembly falls within the realm of PROPORTIONAL REPRESENTATION.

STATE LEGISLATURE
The State Legislature includes both the State Senate and State Assembly and becomes classified as PROPORTIONAL REPRESENTATION.

STATE GOVERNOR'S TRIAG
The Governor deals with the Legislator and is classified as PROPORTIONAL REPRESENTATION.

PRESIDENT'S TRIAG FRAMERS OF THE CONSTITUTION'S AMENDMENT
The President deals with both the Senators (Ambassadors) and the House of Representative and is classified as PROPORTIONAL REPRESENTATION.

PRESIDENT'S TRIAG 17 AMENDMENT
The President deals with both the Senators (Federal Governors) and the House of Representative and becomes classified as NON PROPORTIONAL REPRESENTATION.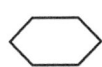

Table of elected officials within the State Governors' Triag systems, the President's Framers of the Constitution's Triag System and President's 17th Amendment Triag System.

State	A State Senate	B State Assembly	C USA Senate or Federal Governor	D USA House	E State Governor	F State Governor's Triag System or Ambassador	G President's Framers of the Constitution's Triag System	H President's 17th Amendment Triag System	I President's Triag Framers of the Constitution's System Minus President's Triag 17th Amendment System
Alabama	35	105	2	7	1	140	148	9	139
Alaska	20	40	2	1	1	60	62	3	59
Arizona	30	60	2	8	1	90	99	10	89
Arkansas	35	100	2	4	1	135	140	6	134
California	40	80	2	53	1	120	174	55	119
Colorado	35	65	2	7	1	100	108	9	99
Connecticut	30	120	2	5	1	150	156	7	149
Delaware	21	35	2	1	1	56	58	3	55
Florida	40	120	2	25	1	160	186	27	159
Georgia	56	180	2	13	1	236	250	15	235
Hawaii	20	50	2	2	1	70	73	4	69
Idaho	35	70	2	2	1	105	108	4	104
Illinois	59	118	2	19	1	177	197	21	176
Indiana	50	100	2	9	1	150	160	11	149
Iowa	50	100	2	5	1	150	156	7	149
Kansas	40	126	2	4	1	166	171	6	165
Kentucky	38	100	2	6	1	138	145	8	137
Louisiana	39	105	2	7	1	144	152	9	143
Maine	35	151	2	2	1	186	189	4	185
Maryland	47	65	2	8	1	112	121	10	111
Massachusetts	40		2	10	1	40	51	12	39
Michigan	38	110	2	15	1	148	164	17	147
Minnesota	67		2	8	1	67	76	10	66
Mississippi	50	122	2	4	1	172	177	6	171
Missouri	34	163	2	9	1	197	207	11	196
Montana	50	100	2	1	1	150	152	3	149

State	A State Senate	B State Assembly	C USA Senate or Federal Governor	D USA House	E State Governor	F State Governor's Triag System or Ambassador	G President's Framers of the Constitution's Triag System	H President's 17th Amendment Triag System	I President's Triag Framers of the Constitution's System Minus President's Triag 17th Amendment System
Nebraska	49		2	3	1	49	53	5	48
Nevada	21	41	2	3	1	62	66	5	61
New Hampshire	24	400	2	2	1	64	67	4	63
New Jersey	40	80	2	13	1	120	134	15	119
New Mexico	42		2	3	1	42	46	5	41
New York	62	150	2	29	1	212	242	31	211
North Carolina	50	120	2	13	1	170	184	15	169
North Dakota	47	94	2	1	1	141	143	3	140
Ohio	33	99	2	18	1	132	151	20	131
Oklahoma	48	101	2	5	1	149	155	7	148
Oregon	30	60	2	5	1	90	96	7	89
Pennsylvania	50	203	2	19	1	253	273	21	252
Rhode Island	38	75	2	2	1	113	116	4	112
South Carolina	46	124	2	6	1	170	177	8	169
South Dakota	35	70	2	1	1	105	107	3	104
Tennessee	33	98	2	9	1	131	141	11	130
Texas	31	150	2	32	1	181	214	34	180
Utah	29	75	2	3	1	104	108	5	103
Vermont	14	148	2	1	1	162	164	3	161
Virginia	40	99	2	11	1	139	151	13	138
Washington	49		2	9	1	49	59	11	48
West Virginia	24	65	2	3	1	89	93	5	88
Wisconsin	33	98	2	8	1	131	140	10	130
Wyoming	30	60	2	1	1	90	92	3	89
Total	1,932	4,435	100	435	50	6,367	6,852	535	6,317

Table E

When the 17th Amendment replaced the United States Constitution Article I; Section 3 (Framers of the Constitution), the President dealings with elected officials drop from 6,852 in column G to 535 in column H. Any decisions the President makes under the 17th Amendment excludes 6,317 in Total of column I elected officials. In fact the union of State Governor's Triag system at 6,367 in column F is much greater than the President's 17th Amendment system Triag at 535 in column H.

When the Governors have a powwow (National Governors Association), there States' interests must be considered when making demands of the Federal Government that might come up at one of their sessions. Table E column F Total number suggest that.

Since Governors get-togethers are few, why not replace Federal Governors with State Ambassadors in the Presidential 17th Amendment Triag. After all that is what our Framers of the Constitution wanted in the first place.

The approach in solving this problem was to use set theory. Rather than mentioning terms like Universal set, subsets and Intersecting sets. The columns of all the displayed tables are a good substitutes. Since all the sets are finite, they become countable (numbers in the columns).

The seriousness of the state that the !7th amendment put the United State Government causes me to go a little bit further to prove a point. Maybe the previous tables of number are not proof enough; therefore, a mathematical model is in order here showing how Federal and State representatives are assigned to their respective district. Drawings in array form are used to clarify the procedure. One can think of the array form as a rectangular mesh conforming to the boundaries of a state and having the width and height as disclosed in the following drawings.

A conformal mapping of the Federal House of Representatives state's boundary and constituency is transformed into a one dimension (m) array. The Federal Government defines k to be the number of House of Representative districts in the State.

DEFINITIONS

P is the state's population.
P' is the total computed population of the state within the one dimensional (k) array.
FC is the contingency within a districts.
FC=P/n where / designates division.
State Government constructs the House of Representative's district using the FC contingency.
The FC contingency and PEOPLE(m) of the k districts will probably be quasi equal.
These k patricians must be contiguous (one side must touch).
This one dimensional (k) array can be employed any where over the topography of the State.
The definition of epsilon is the number of persons left over.

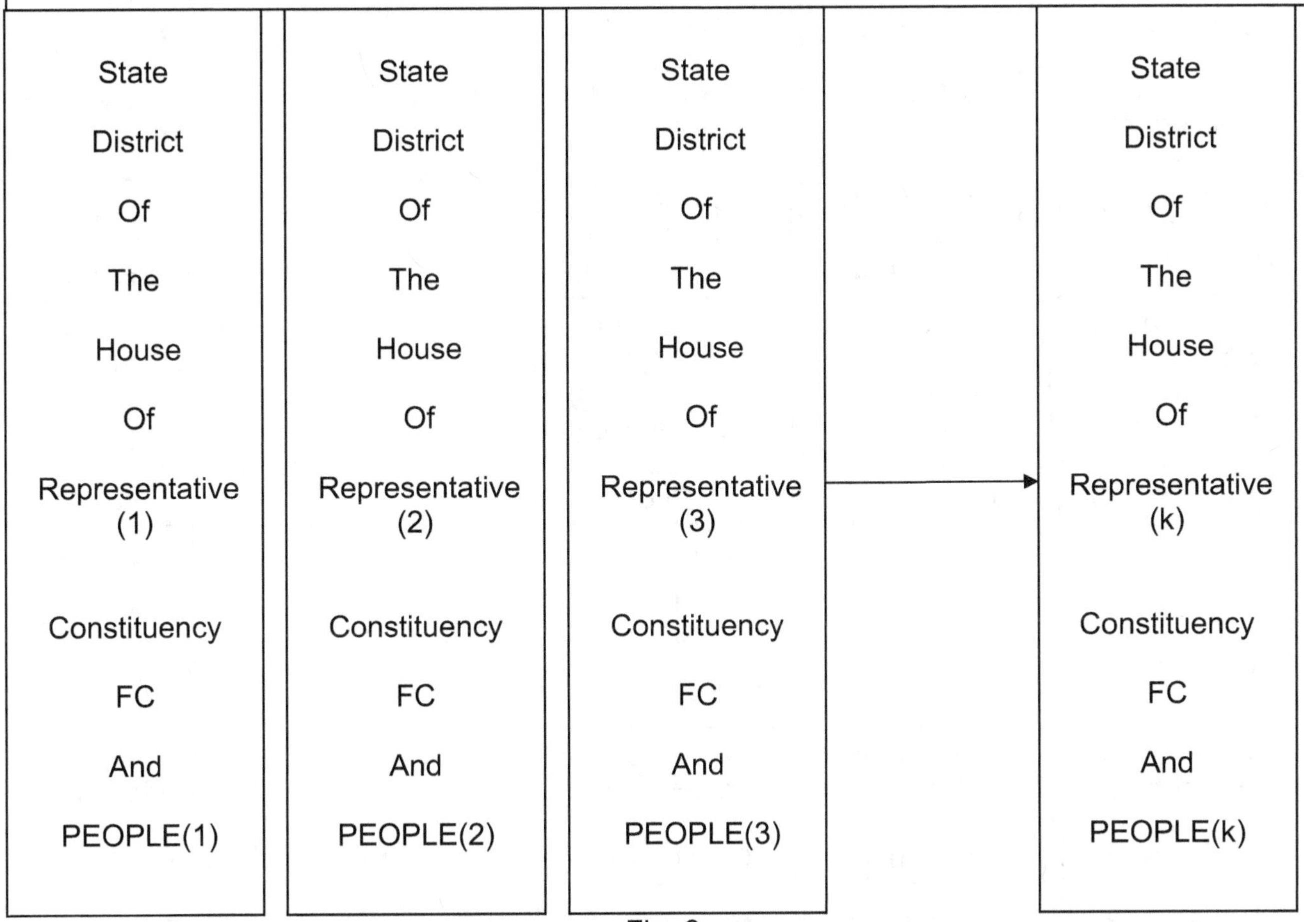

State	State	State		State
District	District	District		District
Of	Of	Of		Of
The	The	The		The
House	House	House		House
Of	Of	Of		Of
Representative (1)	Representative (2)	Representative (3)	⟶	Representative (k)
Constituency	Constituency	Constituency		Constituency
FC	FC	FC		FC
And	And	And		And
PEOPLE(1)	PEOPLE(2)	PEOPLE(3)		PEOPLE(k)

Fig. 6

The whole number summation
P'=PEOPLE(1)+PEOPLE(2)+PEOPLE(3)+++PEOPLE(k)
P=P'+-(plus or minus) epsilon
where epsilon can be ignored using the theory of large numbers.

The Government State Assembly boundary and constituency is transformed into a two dimension (n,m) array.

DEFINITIONS
The State Government chooses the parameters n and m.
This two dimension (n,m) array can be employed any where over the topography of the State.
P is the states population.
SC is the contingency within a State Assembly districts.
SC=P/nxm where / Designates division and x Designates multiplication.
Each state's district uses the SC contingencies to construct the state district.
All PEOPLE(n,m) and the SC contingencies will probably be quasi equal.
SS is the number of State Senators.
SD is the number of State Assembly district in a State Senator's district.
NA is the number of assembly districts.
NA=nxm
The definition of epsilon is the number of persons left over.

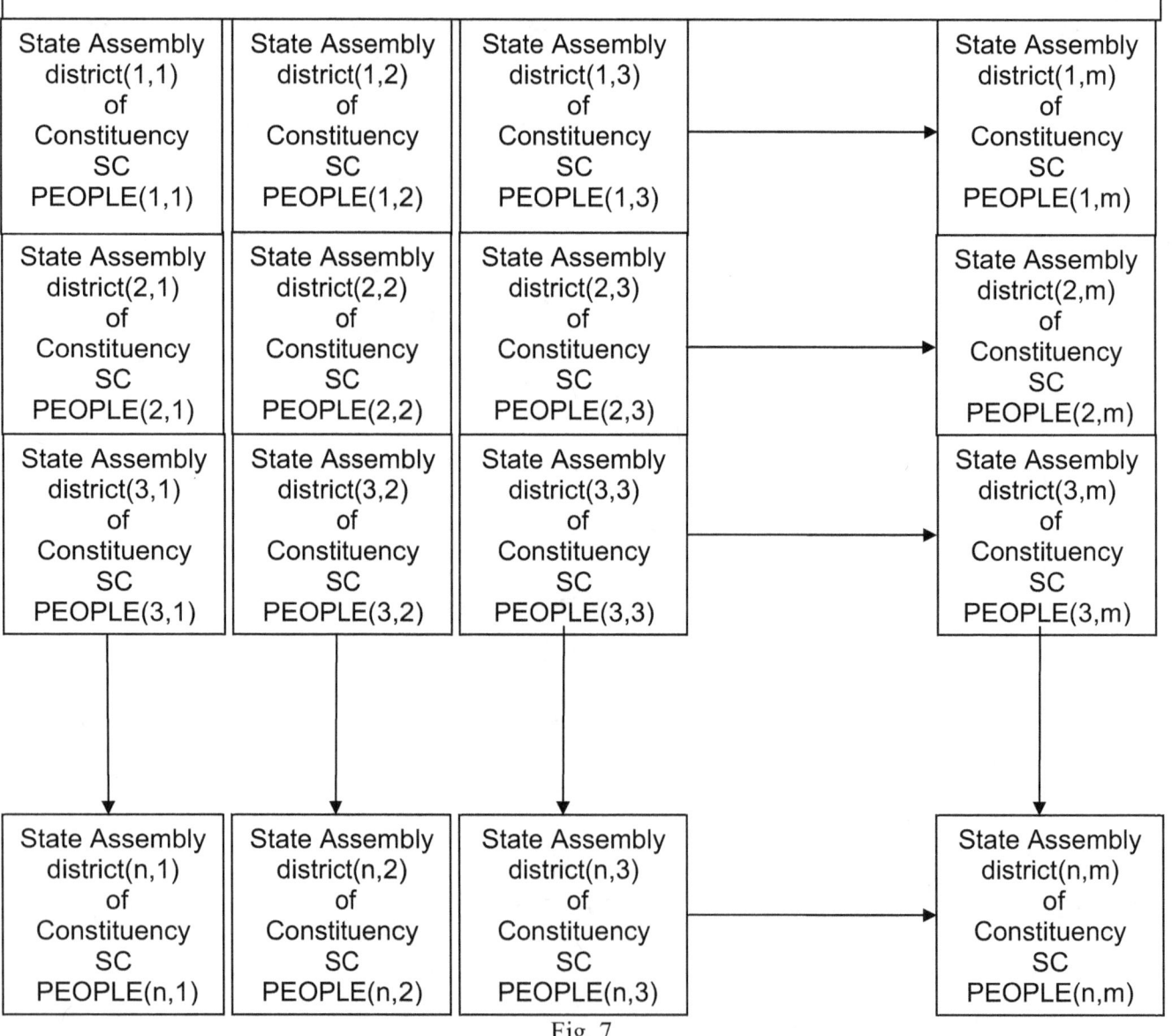

Fig. 7

The whole number summation

SP(!,m)=PEOPLE(1,1)+PEOPLE(1,2)+PEOPLE(1,3)+++PEOPLE(1,m)

SP(2,m)=PEOPLE(2,1)+PEOPLE(2,2)+PEOPLE(2,3)+++PEOPLE(2,m)

SP(3,m)=PEOPLE(3,1)+PEOPLE(3,2)+PEOPLE(3,3)+++PEOPLE(3,m)

SP(n,m)=PEOPLE(n,1)+PEOPLE(n,2)+PEOPLE(n,3)+++PEOPLE(n,m)

P'= SP(!,m)+SP(2,m)+SP(3,m)+++SP(n,m)

P=P'+-(plus or minus) epsilon

where epsilon can be ignored using the theory of large numbers.

SS=nxm/SD

where x designate multiplication, / designates division and SD divides into n or m.

Pick off adjacent State Assembly districts (SD) for each State Senator district (SS).

Lets prove the power of the State Government

PROOF #1

In Fig. 6, k denotes the number of House of Representative districts in the State.

In Fig. 7, let m=k so that the array in Fig. 7 is similar as the one in Fig. 6 displaying k partitions.

From definitions in Fig. 7, substituting m=k

NA=nxk (x designates multiplication)

For n (greater than) >1, the number of State Assembly districts will always be n time greater than the number of Federal House of Representative districts; therefore, there will always be more State Assembly members than Federal House of Representative members throughout the state. The State Government is a better representative of its people than the Federal Government.

PROOF #2

Using the array In Fig. 7, NA=nxm (x designates multiplication) By definition, the State Government chooses the parameters n and m. Going back to the inequality equation (1),
House of Representative {k}<(less than) State Senate {SS}<(less than) State assembly {NA}
The Framers of the Constitution had good reason for recognizing the power of the State Government.

DISENFRANCHISEMENT OF US HOUSE DISTRICTS

State	A	B	C	D
	Population	US Senators (Federal Governors) District NON PROPORTIONAL REPRESENTATIVE m	US House districts PROPORTIONAL REPRESENTATIVE n	The combination of remaining US House districts is the disenfranchisement of constituents within the US Senator (Federal Governors) districts n-m
Alaska	648,818	1	1	0
Delaware DE	817,491	1	1	0
Montana MT	917,621	1	1	0
North Dakota ND	633,837	1	1	0
South Dakota SD	764,309	1	1	0
Vermont VD	619,107	1	1	0
Wyoming WY	501,242	1	1	0
Idaho ID	1,366,332	1	2	1
Maine ME	1,305,728	1	2	1
New Hampshire NH	1,287,687	1	2	1
Rhode Island RI	1,076,164	1	2	1
Hawaii HI	1,257,608	1	2	1
Nebraska NE	1,739,291	1	3	2
Nevada NV	2,241,154	1	3	2
New Mexico NM	1,874,614	1	3	2
Utah UT	2,351,467	1	3	2
West Virginia WV	1,810,354	1	3	2
Arkansas AR	2,725,714	1	4	3
Kansas KS	2,723,507	1	4	3
Mississippi MS	2,881,281	1	4	3
Connecticut CT	3,483,372	1	5	4
Iowa IA	2,944,062	1	5	4
Oklahoma OK	3,511,532	1	5	4
Oregon OR	3,559,596	1	5	4
Kentucky KY	4,117,827	1	6	5
South Carolina SC	4,147,152	1	6	5
Alabama AL	4,500,752	1	7	6
Colorado CO	4,550,688	1	7	6
Louisiana LA	4,496,334	1	7	6
Arizona AZ	5,580,811	1	8	7
Maryland MD	5,508,909	1	8	7
Minnesota MN	5,059,375	1	8	7
Wisconsin WI	501,242	1	8	7
Indiana IN	6,195,643	1	9	8
Missouri MO	5,704,484	1	9	8
Tennessee TN	5,841,748	1	9	8
Washington WA	6,131,445	1	9	8
Massachusetts MA	6,433,422	1	10	9
Virginia VA	7,386,330	1	11	10
Georgia GA	8,684,715	1	13	12
New Jersey NJ	8,638,396	1	13	12
North Carolina NC	8,407,248	1	13	12
Michigan MI	10,079,985	1	15	14
Ohio OH	11,435,798	1	18	17

State	A	B	C	D
	Population	US Senators (Federal Governors) District NON PROPORTIONAL REPRESENTATIVE m	US House districts PROPORTIONAL REPRESENTATIVE n	The combination of remaining US House districts is the disenfranchisement of constituents within the US Senator (Federal Governors) districts n-m
Illinois IL	12,653,544	1	19	18
Pennsylvania PA	12,365,455	1	19	20
Florida FL	17,019,068	1	25	24/
New York NY	19,190,115	1	29	28
Texas TX	22,118,509	1	32	31
California CA	35,484,453	1	53	52
TOTAL	285,275,336	50	435	385

Table F

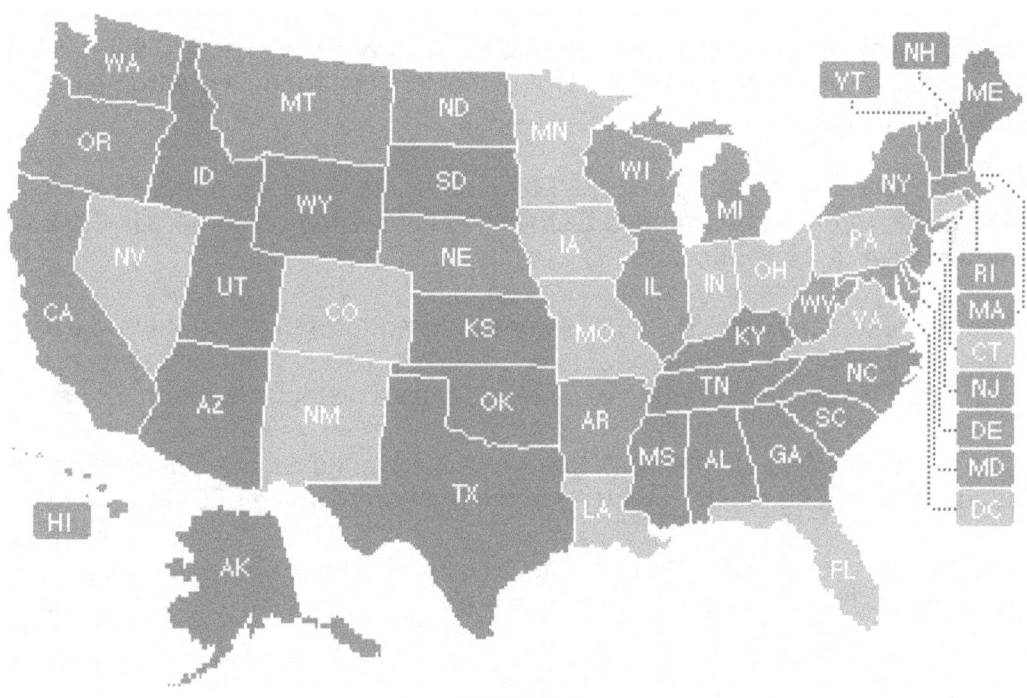

PICTURE A

Each one of the states' boundaries is a United States Senate district and these state boundaries are broken up into one or more United States House of Representative districts; therefore there exists 50 United State Senate districts and 435 United States House of Representative districts. Since the populations of each state is not quasi equal, the combine United States Senate 50 districts are considered to be non proportional representative. Not so with the 435 United States House of Representative districts whose districts were constructed in a proportional representative way resulting in 435 quasi equal populate districts over the entire United States.

Referring to the states, Alaska, Delaware, Montana, North Dakota, South Dakota, Vermont and Wyoming in Table F there exists 1 United States Senate district to 1 House of Representative district. The House of Representative district contains the same population as the United States Senate district in the 7 states. Disenfranchisement equals 0 districts in column D; therefore, disenfranchisement does not exist here.

Referring to the states Idaho, Maine, New Hampshire, Rhode Island and Hawaii there exists 1 United States Senate district to 2 House of Representative districts. Since 2 US House districts are more accurate than 1 Senate District, disenfranchisement is 1 House of Representative district in column D.

Referring to the states Nebraska, Nevada, New Mexico Utah and West Virginia there exists 1 United States Senate district to 3 House of Representative districts. The disenfranchisement is the combination of 2 districts in column D.

Referring to states Arkansas, Kansas and Mississippi there exists 1 United States Senate district to 4 House of Representative districts. The disenfranchisement is the combination of 3 House of Representative districts in column D.

Referring to the states Connecticut, Iowa, Oklahoma and Oregon there exists 1 United States Senate district to 5 House of Representative districts. The disenfranchisement is the combination of 4 districts in column D.

Referring to the states Kentucky and South Carolina there exists 1 United States Senate district to 6 House of Representative districts. The disenfranchisement is the combination of 5 House of Representative districts in column D.

Referring to the states Alabama, Colorado and Louisiana there exists 1 United States Senate district to 7 House of Representative districts. The disenfranchisement is the combination of 6 House of Representative districts in column D.

Referring to the states Arizona, Maryland, Minnesota and Wisconsin there exists 1 United States Senate district to 8 House of Representative districts. The disenfranchisement is the combination of 7 House of Representative districts in column D.

Referring to the states Indiana, Missouri, Tennessee and Washington there exists 1 United States Senate district to 9 House of Representative districts. The disenfranchisement is the combination of the combination of 8 House of Representative districts in column D.

Referring to the state of Massachusetts there exists 1 United States Senate district to 10 House of Representative districts. The disenfranchisement is the combination of 9 districts in column D.

Referring to the state of Virginia, there exists 1 United States Senate district to 11 House of Representative districts. The disenfranchisement is the combination of 10 House of Representative districts in column D.

Referring to the states Georgia, New Jersey and North Carolina, there exists 1 United States Senate district to 13 House of Representative districts. The disenfranchisement is the combination of 12 House of Representative districts in column D.

Referring to the state of Michigan there exists 1 United States Senate district to 15 House of Representative districts. The disenfranchisement is the combination of 14 House of Representative districts in column D.

Referring to the state of Ohio there exists 1 United States Senate district to 18 House of Representative districts. The disenfranchisement is the combination of 17 House of Representative districts in column D.

Referring to the states Illinois and Pennsylvania there exists 1 United States Senate district to 19 House of Representative districts. The disenfranchisement is the combination of 18 House of Representative districts in column D.

Referring to the state of Florida there exists 1 United States Senate district to 25 House of Representative districts. The disenfranchisement is the combination of 24 House of Representative districts in column D.

Referring to the state of New York there exists 1 United States Senate district to 29 House of Representative districts. The disenfranchisement is the combination of 28 House of Representative districts in column D.

Referring to the state of Texas there exists 1 United States Senate district to 32 House of Representative districts. The disenfranchisement is the combination of 31 House of Representative districts in column D.

Referring to the state of California there exists 1 United States Senate district to 53 House of Representative districts. The disenfranchisement is the combination of 52 House of Representative in column E.

DISENFRANCHISEMENT OF STATE HOUSE ASSEMBLY DISTRICTS

State	A United State Senate or Federal Governor District NON PROPORTIONAL REPRESENTATIVE	B State Assembly District PROPORTIONAL REPRESENTATIVE	C The combination of remaining State Assembly districts is the disenfranchisement of constituents within the US Senator (Federal Governors) districts
Delaware	1	35	34
Alaska	1	40	39
New Hampshire	1	40	39
Nevada	1	41	40
Nebraska	1	49	48
Hawaii	1	50	49
Wyoming	1	60	59
Oregon	1	60	69
Arizona	1	60	59
West Virginia	1	65	64
Colorado	1	65	64
Maryland	1	65	64
South Dakota	1	70	69
Idaho	1	70	69
Rhode Island	1	75	74
Utah	1	75	74
New Jersey	1	80	79
California	1	80	79
North Dakota	1	94	93
Wisconsin	1	98	97
Tennessee	1	98	97
Virginia	1	99	98
Ohio	1	99	98
Montana	1	100	99
Arkansas	1	100	99
Iowa	1	100	99
Kentucky	1	100	99
Indiana	1	100	99
Oklahoma	1	101	100
Alabama	1	105	105
Louisiana	1	105	104

State	A United State Senate or Federal Governor District NON PROPORTIONAL REPRESENTATIVE	B State Assembly District PROPORTIONAL REPRESENTATIVE	C The combination of remaining State Assembly districts is the disenfranchisement of constituents within the US Senator (Federal Governors) districts
Michigan	1	110	109
Illinois	1	118	117
Connecticut	1	120	119
North Carolina	1	120	119
Florida	1	120	119
Mississippi	1	122	121
South Carolina	1	124	123
Kansas	1	126	127
Vermont	1	148	147
New York	1	150	149
Texas	1	150	149
Maine	1	151	150
Missouri	1	163	162
Georgia	1	180	179
Pennsylvania	1	203	202
New Mexico	1	none	none
Minnesota	1	none	none
Washington	1	none	none
Massachusetts	1	none	none
TOTAL	50	4,682	4532

Table G

Referring to the state Delaware, there exists 1 United States Senate district to 35 State Assembly districts. Disenfranchisement equals the combination of 34 districts in column C.

Referring to the states Alaska and New Hampshire, there exists 1 United States Senate district to 40 State Assembly districts. Disenfranchisement is the combination of 39 State Assembly district in column C.

Referring to the state Nevada, there exists 1 United States Senate district to 41 State Assembly districts. The disenfranchisement is the combination of 40 districts in column C.

Referring to the state Nebraska , there exists 1 United States Senate district to 49 State Assembly districts. The disenfranchisement is the combination of 48 districts in column C.

Referring to the state Hawaii, there exists 1 United States Senate district to 50 State Assembly districts. The disenfranchisement is the combination of 49 districts in column C.

Referring to states Wyoming, Oregon and Arizona, there exists 1 United States Senate district to 60 State Assembly districts. The disenfranchisement is the combination of 59 State Assembly districts in column C.

Referring to states West Virginia, Colorado and Maryland, there exists 1 United States Senate district to 65 State Assembly districts. The disenfranchisement is the combination of 64 State Assembly districts in column C.

Referring to the states South Dakota and Idaho, there exists 1 United States Senate district to 70 State Assembly districts. The disenfranchisement is the combination of 69 districts in column C.

Referring to the states Rhode Island and Utah, there exists 1 United States Senate district to 75 State Assembly districts. The disenfranchisement is the combination of 74 State Assembly districts in column C.

Referring to the states New Jersey and California, there exists 1 United States Senate district to 80 State Assembly districts. The disenfranchisement is the combination of 79 State Assembly districts in column C.

Referring to the North Dakota, there exists 1 United States Senate district to 94 State Assembly districts. The disenfranchisement is the combination of 93 districts in column C.

Referring to the states Wisconsin and Tennessee, there exists 1 United States Senate district to 98 State Assembly districts. The disenfranchisement is the combination of 97 State Assembly districts in column C.

Referring to the states Virginia and Ohio, there exists 1 United States Senate district to 99 State Assembly districts. The disenfranchisement is the combination of 98 State Assembly districts in column C.

Referring to the states Montana, Arkansas, Iowa, Kentucky and Indiana, there exists 1 United States Senate district to 100 State Assembly districts. The disenfranchisement is the combination of 99 State Assembly districts in column C.

Referring to the State Oklahoma, there exists 1 United States Senate district to 101 State Assembly districts. The disenfranchisement is the combination of 100 districts in column C.

Referring to the states Alabama and Louisiana, there exists 1 United States Senate district to 105 State Assembly districts. The disenfranchisement is the combination of 104 State Assembly districts in column C.

Referring to the states New York and Texas, there exists 1 United States Senate district to 150 State Assembly districts. The disenfranchisement is the combination of 149 State Assembly districts in column C.

Referring to the State Michigan, there exists 1 United States Senate district to 110 State Assembly districts. The disenfranchisement is the combination of 109 districts in column C.

Referring to the State Illinois, there exists 1 United States Senate district to 118 State Assembly districts. The disenfranchisement is the combination of 117 districts in column C.

Referring to the states Connecticut. North Carolina and Florida, there exists 1 United States Senate district to 120 State Assembly districts. The disenfranchisement is the combination of 119 State Assembly districts in column C.

Referring to the State Mississippi, there exists 1 United States Senate district to 122 State Assembly districts. The disenfranchisement is the combination of 121 districts in column C.

Referring to the State South Carolina, there exists 1 United States Senate district to 124 State Assembly districts. The disenfranchisement is the combination of 123 districts in column C.

Referring to the State Kansas, there exists 1 United States Senate district to 126 State Assembly districts. The disenfranchisement is the combination of 125 districts in column C.

Referring to the State Vermont, there exists 1 United States Senate district to 148 State Assembly districts. The disenfranchisement is the combination of 148 districts in column C.

Referring to the State Maine, there exists 1 United States Senate district to 151 State Assembly districts. The disenfranchisement is the combination of 150 districts in column C.

Referring to the State Missouri, there exists 1 United States Senate district to 163 State Assembly districts. The disenfranchisement is the combination of 162 districts in column C.

Referring to the State Georgia, there exists 1 United States Senate district to 180 State Assembly districts. The disenfranchisement is the combination of 179 districts in column C.

Referring to the State Pennsylvania, there exists 1 United States Senate district to 203 State Assembly districts. The disenfranchisement is the combination of 202 districts in column C.

Referring to the whole United States, there exists 50 United States districts to 4,682 State Assembly districts. The disenfranchisement is the combination of 4532 districts in column C.

DISENFRANCHISEMENT OF STATE SENATE DISTRICTS

State	A US Senate or Federal Governor District non proportional representative	B State Senate District proportional representative	C Combination of Remaining State Senate districts is the disenfranchisement of constituents within the US Senator (Federal Governors) districts
Vermont	1	14	13
Alaska	1	20	19
Hawaii	1	20	19
Delaware	1	21	20
Nevada	1	21	20
New Hampshire	1	24	23
West Virginia	1	24	23
Utah	1	29	28
Wyoming	1	30	29
Connecticut	1	30	29
Oregon	1	30	29
Arizona	1	30	29
Texas	1	31	30
Wisconsin	1	33	32
Tennessee	1	33	32
Ohio	1	33	32
Missouri	1	34	33
Arkansas	1	35	34
Alabama	1	35	34
Colorado	1	35	34
Idaho	1	35	34
Maine	1	35	34
South Dakota	1	35	35
Rhode Island	1	38	37
Kentucky	1	38	37

State	A US Senate or Federal Governor District non proportional representative	B State Senate District proportional representative	C Combination of Remaining State Senate districts is the disenfranchisement of constituents within the US Senator (Federal Governors) districts
Michigan	1	38	37
Louisiana	1	39	38
Kansas	1	40	39
Massachusetts	1	40	39
Virginia	1	40	39
New Jersey	1	40	39
Florida	1	40	39
California	1	40	39
New Mexico	1	42	41
South Carolina	1	46	45
North Dakota	1	47	46
Maryland	1	47	46
Oklahoma	1	48	47
Nebraska	1	49	48
Washington	1	49	48
Montana	1	50	49
Mississippi	1	50	49
Iowa	1	50	49
Indiana	1	50	49
North Carolina	1	50	49
Pennsylvania	1	50	49
Georgia	1	56	55
Illinois	1	59	58
New York	1	62	61
Minnesota	1	67	66
TOTAL	50	1,932	1,882

Table H

Referring to the state of Vermont, there exists 1 United States Senate district to 14 State Assembly districts. Disenfranchisement equals the combination of 13 districts in column C.

Referring to the states of Alaska and Hawaii, there exists 1 United States Senate district to 20 State Assembly districts. Disenfranchisement is the combination of 19 State Assembly district in column C.

Referring to the states of Delaware and Nevada, there exists 1 United States Senate district to 21 State Assembly districts. Disenfranchisement is the combination of 20 State Assembly district in column C.

Referring to the states of New Hampshire and West Virginia, there exists 1 United States Senate district to 21 State Assembly districts. Disenfranchisement is the combination of 20 State Assembly district in column C.

Referring to the state of Utah, there exists 1 United States Senate district to 29 State Assembly districts. Disenfranchisement is the combination of 28 districts in column C.

Referring to the states of Wyoming, Connecticut, Oregon and Arizona, there exists 1 United States Senate district to 30 State Assembly districts. Disenfranchisement is the combination of 29 State Assembly district in column C.

Referring to the state of Texas, there exists 1 United States Senate district to 30 State Assembly districts. Disenfranchisement is the combination of 31 districts in column C.

Referring to the states of Wisconsin, Tennessee and Ohio, there exists 1 United States Senate district to 33 State Assembly districts. Disenfranchisement is the combination of 32 State Assembly district in column C.

Referring to the state of Missouri, there exists 1 United States Senate district to 34 State Assembly districts. Disenfranchisement is the combination of 33 districts in column C.

Referring to the states of Arkansas, Alabama, Colorado, Idaho, Maine and South Dakota, there exists 1 United States Senate district to 35 State Assembly districts. Disenfranchisement is the combination of 34 State Assembly district in column C.

Referring to the states of Rhode Island, Kentucky and Michigan, there exists 1 United States Senate district to 38 State Assembly districts. Disenfranchisement is the combination of 37 State Assembly district in column C.

Referring to the state of Louisiana, there exists 1 United States Senate district to 39 State Assembly districts. Disenfranchisement is the combination of 38 districts in column C.

Referring to the states of Kansas, Massachusetts, Virginia, New Jersey, Florida and California, there exists 1 United States Senate district to 40 State Assembly districts. Disenfranchisement is the combination of 39 State Assembly district in column C.

Referring to the state of New Mexico, there exists 1 United States Senate district to 42 State Assembly districts. Disenfranchisement is the combination of 41 districts in column C.

Referring to the state of South Carolina, there exists 1 United States Senate district to 46 State Assembly districts. Disenfranchisement is the combination of 45 districts in column C.

Referring to the states of North Dakota and Maryland, there exists 1 United States Senate district to 47 State Assembly districts. Disenfranchisement is the combination of 46 State Assembly district in column C.

Referring to the state of Oklahoma, there exists 1 United States Senate district to 48 State Assembly districts. Disenfranchisement is the combination of 47 districts in column C.

Referring to the states of Nebraska and Washington, there exists 1 United States Senate district to 49 State Assembly districts. Disenfranchisement is the combination of 48 State Assembly district in column C.

Referring to the states of Montana, Mississippi, Iowa, Indiana, North Carolina and Pennsylvania, there exists 1 United States Senate district to 50 State Assembly districts. Disenfranchisement is the combination of 49 State Assembly district in column C.

Referring to the state of Georgia, there exists 1 United States Senate district to 56 State Assembly districts. Disenfranchisement is the combination of 55 districts in column C.

Referring to the state of Illinois, there exists 1 United States Senate district to 59 State Assembly districts. Disenfranchisement is the combination of 58 districts in column C.

Referring to the state of New York, there exists 1 United States Senate district to 62 State Assembly districts. Disenfranchisement is the combination of 61 districts in column C.

Referring to the state of Minnesota, there exists 1 United States Senate district to 67 State Assembly districts. Disenfranchisement is the combination of 66 districts in column C.

Referring to the whole United States, there exists 50 United States Senate district to 1,932 State Assembly districts. Disenfranchisement is the combination of 1,882 districts in column C.

DESIGNING A STATE ASSEMBLY DISTRICT

Referring to the states, Alaska, Delaware, Montana, North Dakota, South Dakota, Vermont and Wyoming in Table E, once again there exists 1 United States Senate district to 1 House of Representative district. The House of Representative district contains the same population as the United States Senate district in the 7 states. To illustrate, Table I follows.

State	A Population	B US Senate m	C US House n	D State Assembly Districts	E US House Population	F US Senate Population	G Not Disenfranchised n-m
Alaska	648,818	1	1	40	648,818	648,818	0
Delaware	817,491	1	1	35	817,491	817,491	0
Montana	917,621	1	1	100	917,621	917,621	0
North Dakota	633,837	1	1	94	633,837	633,837	0
South Dakota	764,309	1	1	70	764,309	764,309	0
Vermont	619,107	1	1	148	619,107	619,107	0
Wyoming	501,242	1	1	60	501,242	501,242	0

Table I

In Table I column G; disenfranchisement does not exist. The logic that follows can be applied to all states in Table I. The state of Montana is chosen.

The state of Montana has 1 United States Senate district, 1 United States House of Representative district and 100 State Assembly districts.

In Fig. 7, n=1; SC=P/k; and .P=917621. let m=k..

From Fig. 7., Assume the State constructs the State Assembly quasi equal districts in the following sequence.

When adding k State Assembly districts to the state of Montana, the following scenario takes place in Table J that follows.

k	US Senate Population	State Assembly District #	District population SC=P/k	Dispositions	POLL
1	917,621	1	917,621/k	Determinant	^
2	917,621	2	917,621/k	Over Determinant	I
3	917,621	3	917,621/k	Over Determinant	I
"	"	"	"	"	I
"	"	"	"	"	I
"	"	"	"	"	I
100	917,621	100	917,621/k	Over Determinant	I
101	917,621	101	917,621/k	Over Determinant	I
102	917,621	102	917,621/k	Over Determinant	I
"	"	"	"	"	I
"	"	"	"	"	I
"	"	"	"	"	*

k	US Senate Population	State Assembly District #	District population SC=P/k	Dispositions	POLL
917,621	917,621	917,621	1	Very much Over Determinant	Exact Poll exists here! There are 917,621 Districts with 1 constituent in a district

Table J

In Table J, k=P (917,621) SC=1 , there is 1 US Senate district and P (917,621) State Assembly districts. Of course, k=P is Very much over Determinant. As k increases SC decreases.

When k=P (917,621), there are P (917,621) State Assembly districts with one constituent within voting on any issue like is done on election day for candidates (true poll); whereas, 2 United State Senate members will vote on the same issue. Pretty ridiculous! When k=P (917,621) why poll the State Assembly on an issue? The State Assembly is the poll.

In the field of mathematics one negation has to be shown to disprove a theorem (17 Amendment).

Somewhere between k=1 and k=P (917,621) there exists a k number that will allow the Montana State Assembly to be better than taking a poll on any issue. When designing a State Assembly district, the State legislature of Montana should keep this in mind.

The internet can be utilized to poll for that k number on any issue. This is just a suggestion.

The legislature's emails will further increase communication between the state government and its constituents something the US Senators (Federal Governors) don't do.

VOTER DISENFRANCHISEMENT

When the winning candidates are sworn into office, voters don't realize to what extent their votes affect the construction of government. Two tables are brought together as one table to facilitate the comparison between the Framers of the Constitution Amendment and the 17 Amendment. The title at the top of the attached tables describes the voting category of the tables and the number of Y's in each row of the tables.

Tables are presented with the first row made up of the offices of candidates and succeeding rows consists of permutation and combination of possible voter's outcome of choices' made at the voting machine where a voter selects his candidate by ballot. A yes (Y) means at the final vote count the voting person's candidate has won the election and a no (N) means the voting person's candidate has lost the election.

When dealing with the 17 amendment, the tables that follow will show voter disenfranchisement. The proof of ostracizing a voters choice becomes apparent looking at the count column of each table. Refer to the APPENDIX A.

PROOF #1

PRESIDENT'S TRIAD FRAMERS OF THE CONSTITUTION'S AMENDMENT (GOVERNOR EXCLUDED) ONE Y'S COMPRISES SENATE (AMBASSADOR)

PRESIDENT	US ASSEMBLY	STATE SENATOR	STATE ASSEMBLY	COUNT
Y	N	N	N	1
N	Y	N	N	2
N	N	Y	N	3
N	N	N	Y	4

PRESIDENT TRIAD FEDERAL SYSTEM 17 AMENDMENT ONE Y'S COMPRISES SENATE (FEDERAL GOVERNOR)

PRESIDENT	SENATE OR FEDERAL GOVERNOR	US ASSEMBLY	COUNT
Y	N	N	1
N	Y	N	2
N	N	Y	3

In Proof #1 there exist 4 rows of ONE Y'S in President's Triad Framers of the Constitution's Amendment and 3 rows of ONE Y'S in the President Triad Federal System 17 Amendment. The ostracize disenfranchisement is 1.

PRESIDENT'S TRIAD FRAMERS OF THE CONSTITUTION'S AMENDMENT (GOVERNOR EXCLUDED) TWO Y'S COMPRISES SENATE (AMBASSADOR)

PRESIDENT	US ASSEMBLY	STATE SENATOR	STATE ASSEMBLY	COUNT
Y	Y	N	N	1
Y	N	Y	N	2
Y	N	N	Y	3
N	Y	Y	N	4
N	Y	N	Y	5
N	N	Y	Y	6

PRESIDENT TRIAD FEDERAL SYSTEM 17 AMENDMENT TWO Y'S COMPRISES SENATE (FEDERAL GOVERNOR)

PRESIDENT	SENATE OR FEDERAL GOVERNOR	US ASSEMBLY	COUNT
Y	Y	N	1
Y	N	Y	2
N	Y	Y	3

In Proof #2 there exist 6 rows of TWO Y'S in President's Triad Framers of the Constitution's Amendment and 3 rows of TWO Y'S in the President Triad Federal System 17 Amendment. The ostracize disenfranchisement is 3.

PROOF #3

PRESIDENT'S TRIAD FRAMERS OF THE CONSTITUTION'S AMENDMENT (GOVERNOR EXCLUDED) THREE Y'S COMPRISES SENATE (AMBASSADOR)

PRESIDENT	US ASSEMBLY	STATE SENATOR	STATE ASSEMBLY	COUNT
Y	Y	Y	N	1
Y	Y	N	Y	2
Y	N	Y	Y	3
N	Y	Y	Y	4

PRESIDENT TRIAD FEDERAL SYSTEM 17 AMENDMENT THREE Y'S COMPRISES SENATE (FEDERAL GOVERNOR)

PRESIDENT	SENATE OR FEDERAL GOVERNOR	US ASSEMBLY	COUNT
Y	Y	Y	1

In Proof #3 there exist 4 rows of THREE Y'S in President's Triad Framers of the Constitution's Amendment and 1 row of THREE Y'S in the President Triad Federal System 17 Amendment. The ostracize disenfranchisement is 3.

PROOF #4

PRESIDENT'S TRIAD FRAMERS OF THE CONSTITUTION'S AMENDMENT (GOVERNOR EXCLUDED) FOUR Y'S COMPRISES SENATE (AMBASSADOR)

PRESIDENT	US ASSEMBLY	STATE SENATOR	STATE ASSEMBLY	COUNT
Y	Y	Y	Y	1

PRESIDENT TRIAD FEDERAL SYSTEM 17 AMENDMENT FOUR Y'S

PRESIDENT	SENATE OR FEDERAL GOVERNOR	US ASSEMBLY	COUNT
			0

In Proof #4 there exist 1 rows of FOUR Y'S in President's Triad Framers of the Constitution's Amendment and 0 rows of FOUR Y'S in the President Triad Federal System 17 Amendment. The ostracize disenfranchisement is 1.

PROOF #5

ONE Y'S PRESIDENT'S TRIAD FRAMERS OF THE CONSTITUTION'S AMENDMENT (PRESIDENT AND GOVERNOR EXCLUDED) COMPRISES SENATE (AMBASSADOR)

US ASSEMBLY	STATE SENATOR	STATE ASSEMBLY	COUNT
Y	N	N	1
N	Y	N	2
N	N	Y	3

PRESIDENT TRIAD FEDERAL SYSTEM 17 AMENDMENT ONE Y'S COMPRISES SENATE (FEDERAL GOVERNOR)

SENATE OR FEDERAL GOVERNOR	US ASSEMBLY	COUNT
Y	N	1
N	Y	2

In Proof #5 there exist 3 rows of ONE Y'S in President's Triad Framers of the Constitution's Amendment and 2 rows of ONE Y'S in the President Triad Federal System 17 Amendment. The ostracize disenfranchisement is 1.

Proof #6

PRESIDENT'S TRIAD FRAMERS OF THE CONSTITUTION'S AMENDMENT (PRESIDENT AND GOVERNOR EXCLUDED) TWO Y'S COMPRISES SENATE (AMBASSADOR)

US ASSEMBLY	STATE SENATOR	STATE ASSEMBLY	COUNT
Y	Y	N	1
Y	N	Y	2
N	Y	Y	3

PRESIDENT TRIAD FEDERAL SYSTEM 17 AMENDMENT TWO Y'S COMPRISES SENATE (FEDERAL GOVERNOR)

SENATE OR FEDERAL GOVERNOR	US ASSEMBLY	COUNT
Y	Y	1

In Proof #6 there exist 3 rows of two y's in President's Triad Framers of the Constitution's Amendment and 1 rows of two y's in the President Triad Federal System 17 Amendment. The ostracize disenfranchisement is 2.

PROOF #7

PRESIDENT'S TRIAD FRAMERS OF THE CONSTITUTION'S AMENDMENT (PRESIDENT AND GOVERNOR EXCLUDED) THREE Y'S COMPRISES SENATE (AMBASSADOR)

US ASSEMBLY	STATE SENATOR	STATE ASSEMBLY	COUNT
Y	Y	Y	1

PRESIDENT TRIAD FEDERAL SYSTEM 17 AMENDMENT THREE Y'S

SENATE OR FEDERAL GOVERNOR	US ASSEMBLY	COUNT
		0

In Proof #7 there exist 1 rows of three y's in President's Triad Framers of the Constitution's Amendment and 0 row of three y's in the President Triad Federal System 17 Amendment. The ostracize disenfranchisement is 1.

PROOF #8

PRESIDENT'S TRIAD FRAMERS OF THE CONSTITUTION'S AMENDMENT
(PRESIDENT AND US ASSEMBLY EXCLUDED) ONE Y'S COMPRISES SENATE (AMBASSADOR)

GOVERNOR	STATE SENATOR	STATE ASSEMBLY	COUNT
Y	N	N	1
N	Y	N	2
N	N	Y	3

PRESIDENT TRIAD FEDERAL SYSTEM 17 AMENDMENT ONE Y'S COMPRISES SENATE (FEDERAL GOVERNOR)

SENATE OR FEDERAL GOVERNOR	COUNT
Y	1

In Proof #8 there exist 3 rows of one y's in President's Triad Framers of the Constitution's Amendment and 1 rows of one y's in the President Triad Federal System 17 Amendment. The ostracize disenfranchisement is 2.

PROOF #9

PRESIDENT'S TRIAD FRAMERS OF THE CONSTITUTION'S AMENDMENT
(PRESIDENT AND US ASSEMBLY EXCLUDED) TWO Y'S COMPRISES SENATE (AMBASSADOR)

GOVERNOR	STATE SENATOR	STATE ASSEMBLY	COUNT
Y	Y	N	1
Y	N	Y	2
N	Y	Y	3

PRESIDENT TRIAD FEDERAL SYSTEM 17 AMENDMENT TWO Y'S

SENATE OR FEDERAL GOVERNOR	COUNT
	0

In Proof #9 there exist 3 rows of two y's in President's Triad Framers of the Constitution's Amendment and 0 rows of two y's in the President Triad Federal System 17 Amendment. The ostracize disenfranchisement is 3.

PROOF #10

PRESIDENT'S TRIAD FRAMERS OF THE CONSTITUTION'S AMENDMENT
(PRESIDENT AND US ASSEMBLY EXCLUDED) THREE Y'S COMPRISES SENATE (AMBASSADOR)

GOVERNOR	STATE SENATOR	STATE ASSEMBLY	COUNT
Y	Y	Y	1

PRESIDENT TRIAD FEDERAL SYSTEM 17 AMENDMENT THREE Y'S

SENATE OR FEDERAL GOVERNOR	COUNT
	0

In Proof #10 there exist 1 rows of three y's in President's Triad Framers of the Constitution's Amendment and 0 row of three y's in the President Triad Federal System 17 Amendment. The ostracize disenfranchisement is 1.

PROOF #11

PRESIDENT'S TRIAD FRAMERS OF THE CONSTITUTION'S AMENDMENT (GOVERNOR AND US ASSEMBLY EXCLUDED) ONE Y'S COMPRISES SENATE (AMBASSADOR)

PRESIDENT	STATE SENATOR	STATE ASSEMBLY	COUNT
Y	N	N	1
N	Y	N	2
N	N	Y	3

PRESIDENT TRIAD FEDERAL SYSTEM 17 AMENDMENT ONE Y'S COMPRISES SENATE (FEDERAL GOVERNOR)

PRESIDENT	SENATE OR FEDERAL GOVERNOR	COUNT
Y	N	1
N	Y	2

In poof # 11 there exist 3 rows of one y's in President's Triad Framers of the Constitution's Amendment and 2 rows of one y's in the President Triad Federal System 17 Amendment. The ostracize disenfranchisement is 1.

PROOF #12

PRESIDENT'S TRIAD FRAMERS OF THE CONSTITUTION'S AMENDMENT (GOVERNOR AND ASSEMBLY US EXCLUDED) TWO Y'S COMPRISES SENATE (AMBASSADOR)

PRESIDENT	STATE SENATOR	STATE ASSEMBLY	COUNT
Y	Y	N	1
N	Y	Y	2
Y	N	Y	3

PRESIDENT TRIAD FEDERAL SYSTEM 17 AMENDMENT TWO Y'S COMPRISES SENATE (FEDERAL GOVERNOR)

PRESIDENT	SENATE OR FEDERAL GOVERNOR	COUNT
Y	Y	1

In Proof #12 there exist 3 rows of two y's in President's Triad Framers of the Constitution's Amendment and 1 rows of two y's in the President Triad Federal System 17 Amendment. The ostracize disenfranchisement is 2.

PROOF #13

PRESIDENT'S TRIAD FRAMERS OF THE CONSTITUTION'S AMENDMENT (GOVERNOR AND US ASSEMBLY EXCLUDED) THREE Y'S COMPRISES SENATE (AMBASSADOR)

PRESIDENT	STATE SENATOR	STATE ASSEMBLY	COUNT
Y	Y	Y	1

PRESIDENT TRIAD FEDERAL SYSTEM 17 AMENDMENT THREE Y'S

PRESIDENT	SENATE OR FEDERAL GOVERNOR	COUNT
		0

In Proof #13 there exist 1 rows of three y's in President's Triad Framers of the Constitution Father's Amendment and 0 row of three y's in the President Triad Federal System 17 Amendment. The ostracize disenfranchisement is 1.

PROOF #14

PRESIDENT'S TRIAD FRAMERS OF THE CONSTITUTION'S AMENDMENT
(PRESIDENT, GOVERNOR , US ASSEMBLY EXCLUDED) ONE Y'S COMPRISES SENATE (AMBASSADOR)

STATE SENATOR	STATE ASSEMBLY	COUNT
Y	N	1
N	Y	2

PRESIDENT TRIAD FEDERAL SYSTEM 17 AMENDMENT ONE Y'S COMPRISES SENATE (FEDERAL GOVERNOR)

SENATE OR FEDERAL GOVERNOR	COUNT
Y	1

In Proof #14 there exist 2 rows of one y's in President's Triad Framers of the Constitution's Amendment and 1 rows of one y's in the President Triad Federal System 17 Amendment. The ostracize disenfranchisement is 1.

PROOF #15

PRESIDENT'S TRIAD FRAMERS OF THE CONSTITUTION'S AMENDMENT
(PRESIDENT, GOVERNOR , US ASSEMBLY EXCLUDED) TWO Y'S COMPRISES SENATE (AMBASSADOR)

STATE SENATOR	STATE ASSEMBLY	COUNT
Y	Y	1

PRESIDENT TRIAD FEDERAL SYSTEM 17 AMENDMENT TWO Y'S

SENATE OR FEDERAL GOVERNOR	COUNT
	0

In Proof #15 there exist 1 rows of two y's in President's Triad Framers of the Constitution's Amendment and 0 rows of two y's in the President Triad Federal System 17 Amendment. The ostracize disenfranchisement is 1.

The Proofs shows that Senators (Federal Governors) dictate rather than legislate.

The Framers of the Constitution had good reason for recognizing the power of the State Government.

RESCIND 17TH AMENDMENT REASONS

"Abraham Lincoln worried that the "walls" of the constitution would ultimately be leveled by the "silent artillery of time. His fears materialized with the 1913 ratification of the Seventeenth Amendment which eliminated federalism's structural protection, altering the very nature and meaning of federalism."

SUPREME COURT

"The Court, however, recognized that the seventeenth amendment, which provides for the popular election of Senators, may have diminished the influence that state governments have over the federal political process and, thereby, the effectiveness of the states' role in that process."

NATIONAL GOVERNORS ASSOCIATION

"National Governors Association, and others indicate that, perhaps, the State governments made a mistake in passing the seventeenth amendment. The end result of this mistake affected the degree of autonomy the State governments have in exercising their authority and has effectively relegated them to the position of lobbyists. Additionally, Congress, left unchecked by the seventeenth amendment, has now created a national fiscal situation that is fundamentally out of balance."

SENATOR ZELL MILLER

"In 2004, after announcing his retirement, Senator Zell Miller introduced a constitutional amendment that would repeal the Seventeenth Amendment, arguing that it gives too much power to Washington's special interests and was an attack on federalism:"

"Having now jumped off the Golden Gate Bridge of political reality, before I hit the water and go splat, I have introduced a bill that would repeal the 17th amendment. I use the word ``would," not ``will," because I know it doesn't stand a chance of getting even a single cosponsor, much less a single vote beyond my own."

"You see, the reformers of the early 1900s killed it dead and cremated the body when they allowed for the direct election of U.S. Senators."

"Up until then, Senators were chosen by State legislatures, as James Madison and Alexander Hamilton had so carefully crafted."

"Direct elections of Senators, as great and as good as that sounds, allowed Washington's special interests to call the shots, whether it is filling judicial vacancies, passing laws, or issuing regulations. The State governments aided in their own collective suicide by going along with that popular fad at the time."

"Make no mistake about it. It is the special interest groups and their fundraising power that elect Senators and then hold them in bondage forever."

"In the past five election cycles, Senators have raised over $1.5 billion for their election contests, not counting all the soft money spent on their behalf in other ways. Few would believe it, but the daily business of the Senate in fact is scheduled around fundraising."

"Instead of Senators who thoughtfully make up their own minds as they did during the Senate's greatest era of Clay, Webster, and Calhoun, we now have too many Senators who are mere cat's-paws for the special interests. It is the Senate's sorriest of times in its long, checkered, and once glorious history."

"A wise man, that Lincoln, who understood and predicted all too well the fate of our Republican form of government. Too bad we didn't listen to him."

17TH AMENDMENT EFFECTS

- The 17th Amendment caused the Federal Government to go off out of control, seizing the power to govern the people away from the States' Governments.
- The 17th Amendment allow the power to be transferred from States Governments' officials to non-elected Federal Government officials.
- The 17th Amendment altered the balance of power.
- The 17th Amendment creates a relationship combined with the effect of the Supremacy Clause delivers a non returning concentrated power to the Federal Government.
- The 17th Amendment did not reduce or eliminate corruption.
- The 17th Amendment served to alter or rearrange the structure of the Constitution.
- The 17th Amendment created a radical structural change of our original Constitution serving to allow for cunning and conniving individuals to play off the emotions of current public sentiment to seize control of the office of United States Senator (People elected).
- The 17th Amendment upsets the balance of States Governments' rights.
- The 17th Amendment allow an uninformed general public to control both houses of Congress.
- The 17th Amendment created the "modern day" phenomena of blue-ribbon commissions, study-groups and the independent counsel law.
- The 17th Amendment took away from States' Governments their Constitutional role of indirect participation in the Federal Government's process losing "States Rights.".
- Due to the 17th Amendment a centralized and unrestrained Federal Government emerged.
- Due to the 17th Amendment the Supreme Court must protect certain aspects of state sovereignty.
- Due to the 17th Amendment the Supreme Court recognized the diminishing power of States' Governments over the Federal Government.
- Due to the 17th Amendment the balance of power to govern between the States' Governments and the Federal Government disappeared.
- Due to the 17th Amendment there is quite a bit of corruption involved in the election of senators.
- Due to the 17th Amendment a Republic Form of Government became a Democratic form of government.
- Due to the 17th Amendment through States Governments' Legislatures the residents of the States' Governments could not roadblock any existing Federal Government power.
- Due to the 17th Amendment the States' Governments became appendages or franchises of the centralized Federal Government.
- Due to the 17th Amendment the centralized Federal Government becomes a monopoly.
- Due to the 17th Amendment the centralized Federal Government is given the powers of legal counterfeiting money.

- Due to the 17th Amendment produced two independent divisions of power the States' Governments and a centralized Federal Government.
- Due to the 17th Amendment the National Governor's Association is performing the functions of the States Governments Legislatures.
- Due to the 17th Amendment the National Governor's Association with no formal authority is at the mercy of the centralized Federal government.
- Due to the 17th Amendment the centralized Federal Government has been usurping the powers of the States' Governments.
- Due to the 17th Amendment United States Senate (Ambassador) is a clone of the United States House Representatives.
- Due to the 17th Amendment political monetary contribution kick back billions of dollars in tax breaks and land subsidies to special interest groups.
- Due to the 17th Amendment the States Governments have been reduced from an equal partner with the Federal Government to a common lobbyist losing States Sovereignties and State Rights to funded Federal Government mandates like the No Child Left Behind Act with its system of compulsory tests.

ELIMINATING THE 17TH AMENDMENT

- Eliminating the 17th Amendment would include States Governments' Legislatures in the Federal Government's decision making process.
- Eliminating the 17th Amendment would appropriately as needed allow the States Governments Legislatures to decentralize power of the Federal Governments.
- Eliminating the 17th Amendment would give state legislatures direct influence over the selection of federal judges and the jurisdiction of the federal judiciary and much greater ability to modify the power of the federal judiciary.
- Eliminating the 17th Amendment allows the flow of power between the States Governments Legislatures and the Federal Government to flow satisfying the needs of the Republic.
- Eliminating the 17th Amendment allows the States Governments' legislatures to represent the inhabitants of the states' territory.
- Eliminating the 17th Amendment forces the senators (Ambassadors) whom dependent on States Governments' Legislatures for reelection to be vigilant in supporting the States Governments' rights against legislative or executive infringement.
- Eliminating the 17th Amendment allows the States Governments' Legislatures to elect senators (Ambassadors) to create a total defense against Federal Government tyranny.
- Eliminating the 17th Amendment allows the States Governments' Legislatures elected senators (Ambassadors) to give the inhabitance of the States' Governments the means of defending themselves against encroachments of the Federal Government.
- Eliminating the 17th Amendment gives the States' Governments an agency made up of States Governments' Legislatures elected senators (Ambassadors) that will secure the authority of the States' Governments in forming the Federal Government.
- Eliminating the 17th Amendment, States Governments Legislatures would not hesitate to instruct United States senators (Ambassadors) on making voting decisions.
- Eliminating the 17th Amendment brings back the Framers of the Constitution principle of forming a government that deemed the most effective in ensuring freedom, liberty, and equal protection under the law for all.
- Eliminating the 17th Amendment recognizes the will of the people that truly is to be the ultimate end of the function of governments' envisions to best achieve a Republic form of government depending on the vigilance of the governed to work as designed or else having the unique ability to allow the will of its people to peacefully destroy the Republic form of government itself.
- Eliminating the 17th Amendment makes people sovereign, with the States' Governments being next in line.
- Eliminating the 17th Amendment allows the more traditional, level headed method of the States Governments Legislatures to decide to pick the senator as Ambassadors to the Federal Government.

- Eliminating the 17th Amendment indicates that the States Governments' Legislatures are more versed in the law than the population at large and are less likely to be swayed from picking better senatorial candidates for the United States Senate (Ambassadors) allowing the inhabitants of the States' Governments to indirectly participate.
- Eliminating the 17th Amendment, there will exist a Republic form of government where the ultimate power resides with the States Governments' Legislatures and the people within the States' Governments.
- Eliminating the 17th Amendment, there will exist a Republic form of government creating a national sovereignty and States Governments' sovereignties.
- Eliminating the 17th Amendment there will exist a Republic form of government where power will be divided and spread among the Legislative, Judiciary and Executive branches for the solitary reason of proving the highest sovereignty, the individual citizen.
- Eliminating the 17th Amendment would restore both a wholesome Federal Government and bicameralism.
- Eliminating the 17th Amendment would have a dramatic and positive effect on United States Senate (Ambassador) campaign spending.
- Eliminating the 17th Amendment would return to the direct election of United States House of Representative members and indirect States Governments' Legislatures elections of Senators (Ambassador) to the inhabitances of the States' Governments.
- Eliminating the 17th Amendment would allow the States' Governments to lobby for some political ideals that are unseen to the average inhabitants of States' Governments such as disputes between states and interstate commerce regulations.
- Eliminating the 17th Amendment would return the Senate (Ambassador) to its proper role of blocking the rampart combination of decision making between the President and the House of Representatives.
- Eliminating the 17th Amendment, the Senate will act as a bridge between States Governments' Legislatures and the Federal Government referring to issues coming from both directions.
- Eliminating the 17th Amendment restores the Senate (Ambassadors) as a bridge and as a throttle between the States Governments' Legislatures and Federal Government.
- Eliminating the 17th Amendment, the Federal Government will go back to having two chambers of legislatures where the United States Senate (Ambassador) representing the ideals of the States' Governments and United States House of Representatives representing the people will simultaneously serve in the Federal Government.
- Eliminating the 17th Amendment, the United States Senate (Ambassador) would guard States Governments sovereignties from Federal Government's "natural" tendencies to draw authority to itself.
- Eliminating the 17th Amendment, the United States Senate (Ambassador) would decentralize the Federal Government's authority.
- Eliminating the 17th Amendment, the States Governments' Legislatures would have the authority to remove a United States Senator (Ambassador) who does not arbitrate in the business of the people.
- Eliminating the 17th Amendment, the United States Senators (Ambassadors) would not allow the Federal Government to usurp States Governments' sovereignties.
- Eliminating the 17th Amendment will allow States Governments to have input from the Federal Government so as to decide between national and local issues.
- Eliminating the 17th Amendment, States' Governments could escalate issues to the United States Senate (Ambassador) through the States Governments' Legislatures satisfying differences between the States' Governments and the Federal Government.
- Eliminating the 17th Amendment, the Federal Government would gain strength.
- Eliminating the 17th Amendment, the States' Governments would place a leash on the Federal Government doing away with Federal Government's encroachment into the internal affairs of the States' Governments.

- Eliminating the 17th Amendment, the Legislative branch of the United States government will respect the sovereignties of States' Governments and satisfy the desires of the States Governments' inhabitances.
- Eliminating the 17th Amendment, United States Senators (Ambassador) will often discuss the Federal Government affairs with their States Governments' Legislators.
- Eliminating the 17th Amendment, United States Senators (Ambassador) do not need to raise millions of dollars for campaigning for United States Senate seats eliminating elite corporations donations making the United States Senators (Ambassador) beholden to corporations
- Eliminating the 17th Amendment, the Federal Government will discuss the Federal Governments' affairs with the States Governments' Legislatures instead of with elite corporations.
- Eliminating the 17th Amendment, the States Governments' legislatures defends the States' Governments against the encroachments of the federal Government.
- Eliminating the 17th Amendment gives each State Government direct representation in the Legislative branch of the United States government to deter the usurpation of powers that was constitutionally reserved to the States Governments or to the people as stated in the 10th Amendment, the last Amendment to the Bill of Rights.
- Eliminating the 17th Amendment would return the United States Senate (Ambassador) to being a body that represents the States Governments' Legislatures at the Federal Government's level resulting in restoring the checks and balances of power that was originally provided by the Frames of the Constitution.

ATTEMPTS UNITED STATES SENATORS TO APPROACH THE PEOPLE

How many times have you had your U.S. Senator approach you and discuss impending legislation with you? Even though you voted for them, they probably did not contact you once. But how many times do you suppose they contacted Enron about impending legislation. Enron and other corporations financed their campaigns, to the tune of millions of dollars, to get you to vote these senators into office. You can safely bet that your United States Senators discuss impending legislation with these corporations on a routine basis.

How often do United States Senators discuss federal affairs with your state legislator? I am still looking for a state legislator who has been contacted by their United States Senator regarding federal affairs. Prior to the enactment of the 17th Amendment to the United States Constitution the U.S. Senators discussed federal affairs with their state legislators on a regular basis. At that time United States Senators did not have to raise millions of dollars to run for office. They were not beholden to the large corporations.

There is no way our United States Senators are going to personally discuss federal affairs with, and handle the input from, 900,000 people. The only choice we have before us is to have them discuss our federal affairs with the State Legislatures as opposed to the large corporations. As originally included in the United States. Constitution, the people of the states will continue to enjoy the right to vote for their United States Representatives.

In 1791 the state legislatures ran the United States Senate, but the 17th Amendment passed in 1913, reversed the power of the states, removing their control over Washington and creating two separate and redundant Houses of the People..

The 17th Amendment did more than increase the role of the federal government. It fundamentally changed the Constitution because it ended the states legislative role in Washington.

In the original design by the Framers of the U.S. Constitution, there was an effective check on Congress through the state legislatures' power to appoint (and remove) United States Senators. The 17th Amendment eliminated the checks and balances available to the states over federal power or over Congress itself in any area.

ATTEMPTS TO RESCIND THE 17TH AMENDMENT

Montana bill SJ-10, to repeal the 17th Amendment, earlier in 2003 passed the Judiciary Committee 6-3 but was defeated in the full Senate Encouragement from Montana residents will be needed to pass the bill in the 2005 session.

Tuesday, February 13, 2007
Utah Senate Bill SB202
The central components to Utah Bill SB202 put forward by Chief Sponsor Howard A Stephenson:

The General Description: This bill addresses issues related to the 17th Amendment to the United States Constitution and permits the Legislature to give direction to certain United States Senators and to receive certain reports from them.

Highlighted Provisions:

This bill:

- allows the Legislature to give formal direction to a United States Senator elected from Utah:
- allows the Legislature to direct a United States Senator elected from Utah to report to the Legislature on certain issues determined by the Legislature:
- provides that any direction or reporting requirements be made by:
- a joint resolution of the Legislature; or
- a written statement, called "The Sense of the Legislature," that contains the signatures of a majority of members of the House and a majority of members of the Senate; and
- directs the Office of Legislative Research and General Counsel to maintain a record of all resolutions, statements, and responses issued under this section.
- Comment: It's fairly obvious that the United States Senate has become a media circus where individual Senators do more to profile themselves rather than represent their states. This bill would hold the Senators "feet to the fire" and make each accountable to the needs of the state. Hopefully, the citizenry would have a clear record to each senator's performance. I wish Senator Stephenson and the other co-sponsors the best of luck and I hope this is enacted in Utah. The next step would be the repeal of the 17th Amendment

REPUBLIC FORM OF GOVERNMENT
THE IDEALS OF THE STATES GOVERNMENTS' LEGISLATURES

The States Governments' Legislatures made up of a State Senate and State Assembly pick the two United States Senators (ambassadors); therefore, the following are statements of the ideals of the States Governments' Legislatures and the people at large through the action of United States Senate (ambassadors) within the Federal Government:

- The United States Senate (ambassadors) is the instrument that restricts Federal Government encroachment of the States' Governments.
- The United States Senate (ambassadors) protects the States' Governments from the Federal Government's encroachment.
- The United States Senate (ambassadors) preserves the structure of the Republic.
- The United States Senate (ambassadors) plays in keeping the balance of power between the States' Governments and the Federal Government allowing the power to shift as to fulfill the requirements of the Republic.
- The United States Senate (ambassadors) makes the States' Governments a Federal Government partner in the Republic.
- The United States Senate (ambassadors) voting actions frustrates corporate lobbyist and other special interest groups.
- The United States Senate (ambassadors) decision-making puts an end to corporate lobbyist and other special interest groups that distort legislation within the Federal Government.
- The United States Senate (ambassadors) discourages Federal Government's expansion that might take away States Governments' authorities and Constitutional rights.
- The United States Senate (ambassadors) predominately adheres to the objectives and goals of the States' Governments.
- The United States Senate (ambassadors) has the power to veto or monitor all three branches of Government (legislative, executive and judicial) within the Republic.
- The United States Senate (ambassadors) approves each piece of legislation, all judicial appointees and all executive appointments.

- The United States Senate (ambassadors) approves all treaties and all military affairs; therefore, the States' Governments takes part in all Federal Government affairs protecting the States Governments' sovereignties.
- The United States Senate (ambassadors) participates in all Federal Government affairs.
- The United States Senate (ambassadors) checks the size of Federal Government.
- The United States Senate (ambassadors) resists delegating power to the Federal Government.
- The United States Senate (ambassadors) is the crossroads of power safeguarding against the Federal Government's encroachment.
- The United States Senate (ambassadors) is the lobbyist to the Federal Government.
- The United States Senate (ambassadors) influences the selection of federal judges, the jurisdiction of the federal judiciary and the ability to modify federal court orders.
- The United States Senate (ambassadors) discourages the Federal Government's bad behavior.
- The United States Senate (ambassadors) restrains the tyrannical tendency of the Federal Government acting as a barrier towards dictatorship.
- The United States Senate (ambassadors) gives to States' Governments an organization that aids in forming the Federal Government and secures the authority of the States' Governments.
- The United States Senate (ambassadors) is vigilant of citizens' rights.
- The United States Senate (ambassadors) is vigilant of Federal Government infringement policies against any State Government.
- The United States Senate (ambassadors) adjusts the flow of power between the States' Governments and the Federal Government to the requirements of the Republic.
- The United States Senate (ambassadors) give the States Governments' constituents a role to play in a Republic to protect the State Government from the Federal Government's encroachment, to create and to preserve the structure of the Republic.
- The United States Senate (ambassadors) upgrades the States' Governments from a lobbyist to being a Federal Government partner in the Republic.
- The United States Senate (ambassadors) give the citizens of the States' Governments a means of defending themselves against encroachments of the Federal Government.
- The United States Senate (ambassadors) stays above the influences of special interest groups.
- The United States Senate (ambassadors) contains the political instrument to advice and give consent to the Presidents' treaties and judicial officers' appointments.
- The United States Senate (ambassadors) differing in member election's method then the United States House of Representative provides a balance in governing power.
- In the preceding statements, States Governments' Legislatures and the words "people at large" could correctly, in most statements. replace the words United States Senate (ambassadors).

A DEMOCRATIC FORM OF GOVERNMENT

Losing States Governments' sovereignties and people's rights begin with the passing of the 17th Amendment resulting in doing away with the States Governments' Legislatures appointment of United States senators favoring the popular election of them.

- Members of the Governor's staff whom represent the concerns of the States' Governments reside in Washington DC to deal with the Federal Government.
- The Federal Government is a pure monopoly resulting in a non existent citizen sovereignty.
- The Federal Government ignores the wishes of the great majority of citizens with reckless and disastrous abandonment.
- Excessive Federal Government exists in the manner of federal deficit spending, inappropriate federal mandates, and the evaporation of state influence over national policy.
- The size of the Federal Government increases.
- The Federal Government creates growth with grant programs due to United States Senate (People elected) participation.
- In order to do business with the Federal Government, all the state's government have facilities in Washington DC.
- Ultimate power in a Democratic form of Government does not reside with the people.

- In a Democratic form of Government, the Supreme Court has to fill a void in the fundamental structure of the Constitution to protect States Governments' sovereignties and people's rights
- The United States of America is a Democracy consisting of two independent Governments a States' Governments and a Federal Government
- Campaign financing is needed for United States Senate (People elected) seats.
- The average cost of a United States Senate (People elected) seat is over five million dollars, probably, spending as much as fifteen or twenty million dollars.
- Alliances are created with corporations and special interests groups during senators' (People elected) elections.
- The United States Senate (People elected) is an independent political body with dictatorial powers.
- Exorbitant expenditures, alliances with well financed lobby groups and electioneering sleights of hand continue to characterize United States Senate (People elected) campaigns.
- A disappointing reality is the vaulting financial reforms of political campaigns to elect senators (People elected) allowing the river of special interest monies to flow between the senators (People elected) and the lobbyist of elite corporations.
- Senators (People elected) use political machines to organize voters and raise money to run statewide popular campaigns.
- A group of senators (People elected) might dictate rather than legislate resulting in trying to gain control of the Democratic form of Government.
- Senators (People elected) might rely on popular opinion polls in determining the course of national policy.
- Tremendous power of the mass media on the senators (People elected) may influence their individual deliberations.
- United State House of Representatives districts are disenfranchised within the United States Senate (People elected) districts.
- Huge concentrations of business, capital, and labor introduces the senators (People elected) to elite corporations diminishing the significance of the individual citizen.
- Voters are disenfranchised within the United States Senate (People elected) districts.
- To select a senator (People elected), voters rely on newspapers, political gossip among friends, public debates, TV talk shows, radio broadcasts and TV telephone call ins.
- Incumbent senators (People elected) use the federal supported TV stations to make appearances an advantage not available to their adversaries.
- Corruption may exist in the election of a senator (People elected).
- It takes six years to unseat a corrupted senator (People elected).
- With the help of a skillful staff corrupted senators (People elected) can stay in office for many years.
- Not to alienate an audience the senator (People elected) candidate tends to telling constituents what they want to hear or he speaks in broad terms.
- Incumbent senators (People elected) use loyal party supporters and States' Governments job appointees to "get out the vote."
- The senator (People elected) might make train whistle-stops, attend barbecues and have thirty second spots on prime time television.
- In an era of increasing interstate commerce, there exists development groups whose procurement of special interest legislation is made easy across state lines through the United States Senate (People elected) .
- Power is transferred to non elected and appointed Federal Government officials whom are not accountable to the constituencies of the States' Governments.
- Out of control, appointed official do not restore the lost accountability to the States' Governments and States Governments' constituencies taking away both the States' sovereignties and the peoples' sovereignties and rights. Bicameralism (State Government and Federal Government) is done away within a Democratic form of Government.

- Federal Government intrusion of States' Governments occurs when illegal immigration, extensive granting of visas and green cards are allowed to satisfy the appetites of corporation in order to great a large, cheap, labor market within the United States.
- The United States Senate (People elected) often deadlock or stalemate the of confirming federal judges.
- The Federal Government is given the powers of legal counterfeiting (making money).
- The liberal interpretations of the commerce clause allows the Federal Government to preempt regulatory areas formerly left to the States' Governments and the States' Governments ability to tax.
- Expanding Federal Government services, the Federal Government makes demands on States' Governments.
- The States' Governments have to comply with the Federal Government's taxing power.
- The Federal Government has the power to incur deficit spending without interruption of States' Governments.
- States' Governments have to adopt Federal Government requirements in order to qualify for Federal Government assistance.
- In education, the Federal Government forces States' Governments to meet federal guidelines on student performance.
- Governors are forced to be lackeys for the Federal Government serving cabinet members and executive branch officials.
- States' Governments do not influence the Federal Government or Supreme Court.
- Check and balance do not exists between States' Governments and Federal Government.
- A change of the balance of power exists between the States' Governments and Federal Government.
- In a Democratic Government, the Federal Government is out of control usurping the States' Governments power over the people.
- The Federal Government has more power than the States' Governments contrary to the aims of the Framers of the Constitution.
- For States' Governments to design and implement programs become often limited.
- Since governors play both personal and institutional roles, he/she must try to protect the States Governments Constitutionals' rights. The governors are reduce to chairmanships roles in the National Association of Governors.
- The two houses of Federal Government have the same constituency to facilitate the creation of logrolling agreements across the non proportional representative United States Senate (People elected) and the proportional representative United States House of Representatives.
- There are two independent Governments a States' Governments and a Federal Government
- A group of senators (People elected) might dictate rather than legislate resulting in trying to gain control of the Government
- Bicameralism (State Government and Federal Government) is done away within a Democratic Government.

STRATEGIES TO RESCIND THE 17TH AMENDMENT
STRATEGY

The 17th Amendment to the United States Constitution can be rescinded by the states alone. State legislatures must be convinced to rescind it. This is not as formidable a task as it appears. Bear with us, and we will outline the strategy. Fortunately there are powerful tools at our disposal. Foremost is the 10th Amendment of the Constitution which declares as follows:

The powers not delegated to the United States by the Constitution, nor prohibited by it to the States, are reserved to the States respectively, or to the people.

In clear and unambiguous language the Constitution asserts that the powers the Federal Government may exercise are those powers delegated to it by the states and people. All other powers, or powers not delegated, are retained by the states and people. In plain, simple language the Federal Government derives all its powers from the Constitution and without it has no power whatsoever to do anything. In other words if the Constitution became abrogated the Federal

Government would cease to exist since it was created by the Constitution. On the other hand the various states of the Union will continue to exist with or without the Constitution, which was created by the states and people. The states and people are therefore supreme as reiterated by the 10th Amendment.

Reviewing delegated powers the U.S. Supreme Court in United States v. Hudson 7 Cranch 32, 33 (1812) affirmed as follows: "The powers of the general government are made up of concessions from the several states; whatever is not expressly given to the former, the latter expressly reserve." This decision was unanimous. Most of the justices on this court were part of the original Supreme Court. They were present when the Constitution was drafted, and many of them participated in drafting it. The case has withstood the test of time having been cited in judicial decisions for nearly 200 years.

Article V of the Constitution sets forth the procedure for adding new amendments, but there is no procedure for rescinding existing amendments. Since the Constitution is silent, the states alone may exercise this reserved power which was not delegated. Therefore, the states have the plenary power to rescind amendments. The exception is the first ten amendments or Bill of Rights, which cannot be rescinded. If 13 states decided the 17th Amendment should be rescinded and passed resolutions accordingly, for example, the amendment would be effectively abrogated, since three fourths of the states would no longer support it as required. The states alone may determine the procedure for rescinding this amendment.

The 17th Amendment is a special case and even one state can overturn it. In Article V which sets forth the procedure for new amendments to the Constitution, there is an express limitation on the amending process as follows: " ... no State, without its consent, shall be deprived of its equal suffrage in the Senate." In this connection James Madison in Federalist Papers #43 writes as follows:

"The prohibition against the adoption of any amendment whereby a state is deprived of its equal suffrage in the Senate without its consent involves two things: first, that if the state chooses to consent, it may be deprived of its equal suffrage in the Senate; and, second, that it may not, by any amendment, be deprived of its power to give or refuse its consent."

Madison's comments were quoted verbatim by the U.S. Supreme Court in Leser v. Garnett 66 L. Ed. 505, 506 (1922), giving great weight and validity to this referenced quotation. There are 12 states which never consented to the ratification of the 17th Amendment and are therefore not subject to it, since no state can " ... be deprived of its power to ... refuse its consent." In other words the 17th Amendment cannot be imposed upon the states which did not consent to it, and a state must expressly consent to any change involving its suffrage in the Senate. If these dissenting states choose to regain their senators and require them to vote the will of the legislature in the U.S. Senate, no amendment can deprive it. Realistically if a few states gained back their suffrage in the Senate, or even if one state accomplished it, the 17th Amendment would become so destabilized that it would collapse.

There are two examples of states rescinding ratifications of constitutional amendments. New Jersey ratified the 14th Amendment and later rescinded its consent before the amendment was adopted. In similar fashion the states of Idaho, Kentucky, Tennessee and West Virginia rescinded their ratifications of the proposed Equal Rights Amendment. The proponents of those amendments were unable to judicially overturn these rescissions. In ratifying or rescinding amendments the federal courts have little or no jurisdiction and are unable to defeat the will of a state legislature.

We have saved the best for last. By a strange quirk of fate the 17th Amendment was never ratified by the legislatures of three fourths of the states as the Constitution requires. The proposed amendment was not popular with state legislators, and there was much balking. Several of the states submitted their ratifications with reservations and provisos. This alone would invalidate their ratifications, since a proposed constitutional amendment must be accepted or rejected with no alterations to the language. After much arm twisting the amendment was declared ratified by the legislatures of 36 states, the minimum then required to amend the Constitution. One of the states counted in the ratification was Ohio. However, Ohio was not a state on May 31, 1913 when the 17th Amendment was declared ratified. Ohio was a U.S. Territory. Therefore the 17th Amendment was ratified by the legislatures of 35 states and one territory, making it an invalid amendment. See Public Law 204 (H.J. Res. 121; August 7, 1953).

A brief digression is in order. In 1787 Congress enacted the Northwest Ordinance, which established autonomous territories of which Ohio was a part. The ordinance provided that any territory therein could voluntarily apply for statehood. Before the Civil War there had been two movements within Ohio Territory for statehood.

Both times the people of Ohio elected to remain a territory, so no application for statehood was filed with the United States. When the Civil War began, Ohio was still listed as a territory of the United States. Ohio fervently supported the Union and raised an army which ultimately reached 200,000 men known as the Ohio Volunteers, which fought fiercely against the Confederacy. In addition Ohio contributed money, horses and sustenance to the Union cause. President Lincoln remarked that the North cannot win the Civil War without the outstanding contributions of Ohio.

In 1862 a new movement for statehood was circulating within Ohio Territory. Since the native sons of Ohio were valiantly fighting for the Union cause, Congress passed a resolution allowing Ohio to send two senators and a congressman to Washington pending ratification of statehood. The South had bolted leaving many vacant seats in Congress. For the third time, however, the people of Ohio rejected statehood, so no statehood application was ever filed with Washington. After the assassination of President Lincoln, the end of the Civil War and the era of Reconstruction everyone forgot about Ohio, which continued to send senators and representatives to Washington.

In 1953 the Library of Congress sponsored a statehood exhibit to commemorate the states. It was discovered Ohio had not made application for statehood. Moreover Ohio statehood had never been conferred. Ohio was not a state. Congress was quickly notified. A few senators deemed this a constitutional crisis, wanted to notify the governors of all the states and put all state legislatures in emergency session to resolve the crisis. Rather than alert the nation, Congress elected to meet in quiet and enacted Public Law 204, which purports to admit Ohio into the Union and back date its admission to March 1, 1803, the date when the people of Ohio rejected the first proposal for statehood. This clouds the validity of the 17th Amendment, which was declared ratified on May 31, 1913.

A grass roots movement which will approach legislators in several states and urge them to rescind the 17th Amendment is urgently needed. Once a few states pass rescission resolutions, it will quickly accelerate, since this will become a popular trend. There are many disgruntled states, and the mood is right for this movement. To implement it assembling a coalition of groups urging rescission will assure success. For example, organized labor has suffered greatly from such things as NAFTA, WTO, free trade ... etc., which have all been enacted by our kept Senate where the states have no vote. Coincidentally labor unions are powerful within the several states but have very little power or influence in Washington. Should labor unions be shown that they can gain great influence in the U.S. Senate by having senators once again appointed by state legislatures, rescinding the 17th Amendment will become a slam dunk. Needing the 17th Amendment to advance their agendas, the proponents of global governance, free trade and loss of our sovereignty have immense power in Washington but have little or no power in state legislatures where labor unions are extremely powerful in many states. Another example is the National Rifle Association, which has its power base within states. Gun control is primarily imposed from the top down, and doing away with the 17th Amendment would benefit the NRA. There are other groups which can be enlisted into the coalition to advance the goal of unraveling the 17th Amendment.

In overturning the 17th Amendment the legislatures of the states of Alabama, Delaware, Louisiana, Mississippi, Rhode Island, South Carolina and Utah would be a great place to begin. These are some of the states which rejected ratification of the 17th Amendment and are apt to consider the proposition. Other states which are good candidates include Alaska, Hawaii, Idaho, Iowa, Nevada and Montana. A state court challenge may succeed especially in one of these states. The federal courts are an improper forum and must be avoided for reasons too numerous to cite here.

If you have a judicial bent and want to raise the issues, you can contact us at Legal for our input. These issues have never before been raised, and anyone raising them will certainly become a legal trail blazer. All that is needed is to convince a state court that the 17th Amendment is not mandatory and may be set aside if the legislature chooses. In the alternative a decision that the 17th Amendment was never ratified would do nicely. Either or both would be a court victory which would begin unraveling the 17th Amendment.

We must convince the states to take back their sovereignties. The Government of the United States is no longer the government of the states and people.

why should we repeal the 17th amendment and forfeit our right to vote for u.s. senators?

How many times have you had your U.S. Senator approach you and discuss impending legislation with you? Even though you voted for them, they probably did not contact you once. But how many times do you suppose they contacted Enron about impending legislation. Enron and other corporations financed their campaigns, to the tune of millions of dollars, to get you to vote these senators into office. You can safely bet that your U.S. Senators discuss impending legislation with these corporations on a routine basis.

How often do U.S. Senators discuss federal affairs with your state legislator? I am still looking for a state legislator who has been contacted by their U.S. Senator regarding federal affairs.

Prior to the enactment of the 17th Amendment to the U.S. Constitution the U.S. Senators discussed federal affairs with their state legislators on a regular basis. At THAT time U.S. Senators did not have to raise millions of dollars to run for office. They were not beholden to the large corporations.

There is no way our U.S. Senators are going to personally discuss federal affairs with, and handle the input from, 900,000 people. The only choice we have before us is to have them discuss our federal affairs with the State Legislatures as opposed to the large corporations. As originally included in the U.S. Constitution, the people of the states will continue to enjoy the right to vote for their U.S. Representatives.

SENATE JOINT RESOLUTION 10 – REPEAL THE 17TH AMENDMENT

Prior to the adoption of the 17th Amendment to the United States Constitution, the United States Senators were elected by the State Legislatures. According to the U.S. Constitution, Article 1, Section 3, Clause 1:

The Senate of the United States shall be composed of two Senators from each State, chosen by the Legislature thereof, for six Years; and each Senator shall have one Vote.

At the time the Constitution was written, the U.S. Representatives were to represent the people and were to be elected by popular vote. The U.S. Senators were to represent the States and were to be elected by the State Legislatures.

The 17th Amendment changed the United States Constitution and took away the States representation in our United States government. It states:

The Senate of the United States shall be composed of two Senators from each State, elected by the people thereof, for six years; and each Senator shall have one vote. The electors in each State shall have the qualifications required for electors of the most numerous branch of the State legislatures.

When vacancies happen in the representation of any State in the Senate, the executive authority of such State shall issue writs of election to fill such vacancies: Provided, That the legislature of any State may empower the executive thereof to make temporary appointments until the people fill the vacancies by election as the legislature may direct.

This amendment shall not be construed as to affect the election or term of any Senator chosen before it becomes valid as part of the Constitution.

Since Representatives in the House are elected by the general population of a state, they represent the individual citizens of the state. People have different anxieties and desires as individuals than they do collectively as a state. In fact, most individual citizens are not even aware of what the state must do to protect its people and their rights.

WHY SHOULD WE REPEAL THE 17TH AMENDMENT?

There are 2 main reasons to repeal the 17th Amendment. These reasons are: Campaign Finance Reform and to protect States' Rights.

CAMPAIGN FINANCE REFORM

:According to Molly Ivins, a columnist for the Fort Worth Star Telegram:

The sad state of the union is that money talks and public policy is sold to the highest bidder. Less than one-tenth of 1 percent of the U.S. population gave 83 percent of all campaign contributions in the 2002 elections. Those who give money in political contributions get back billions in tax breaks, subsidies and the right to exploit public land at ridiculously low prices. This system in turn costs ordinary Americans billions of dollars, not to mention the costs to health, safety and the environment, and the cost of not having enough money for good schools. For example, the top corporations that paid zero taxes from 1996 to 1998 included AT&T, Bristol-Myers Squibb, Chase Manhattan, Enron, Exxon Mobil, General Electric, Microsoft, Pfizer and Phillip Morris. They gave $150.1 million to campaigns from 1991 to 2001. Public Campaign reports they got $55 billion in tax breaks from 96 to 98 alone, perennial legislation to gut the alternative minimum tax and billions in rebates to select corporations.

Right here in Montana, in the race for Senate between incumbent Max Baucus and challenger Mike Taylor, millions of dollars were spent. Max Baucus raised and spent $6.7 million and Mike Taylor raised and spent 1.8 million. Much of this money came from out of state. Some of the contributions came from: American International Group, Microsoft Corporation, General Electric, Goldman Sachs, Bank of America, JP Morgan, Chase & Co., Merck & Company, AOL Time Warner, Blue Cross/Blue Shield, National Pro-Life Alliance, National Rifle Association and Retamco Oil and Gas.

With the original Constitutional provisions before the 17th Amendment, the U.S. Senate was to be a check on Congress to prevent them from dipping into the National treasury to buy votes. But since the passage of the 17th Amendment, rather than being appointed by the State Legislatures, they too must run expensive election campaigns and, instead of checking the problem, they are now part of the problem.

PROTECTING STATES' RIGHTS

James Madison thought that the States should be active participants in the Federal Government. He said:

Whenever power may be necessary for the national government, a certain portion must be necessarily left with the states, it is impossible for one power to pervade the extreme parts of the United States so as to carry equal justice to them. The state legislatures also ought to have some means of defending themselves against the encroachments of the national government. In every other department we have studiously endeavored to provide for its self-defense. Shall we leave the states alone un-provided with the means for this purpose? And what better means can be provided than by giving them some share in, or rather make them a constituent part of, the national government?

Since the enactment of the 17th Amendment, the states have been reduced from an equal l partner with the Federal Government to a common lobbyist, which has resulted with the loss of State Sovereignty, State Rights and a host of Federal mandates some funded and some unfunded. These mandated include the No Child Left Behind Act with its system of compulsory tests.

The other day I heard Eric Feaver, the lobbyist for MEA/MFT, state that he couldn't understand how any U.S. Senator representing Montana could vote to eviscerate the Montana Constitution. He was talking about the act of our U.S. Senators passing the No Child Left Behind Act. This act might sit well with that portion of the public who are not involved in > politics. But if we, as members of the Montana Legislature, had any say in the matter, we would have insisted it did not do harm to the Montana Constitution or to our state government.

It was recently brought to my attention that Governor Martz is proposing hiring a lobbyist in Washington D.C. in order to protect our state's interests. Prior to the adoption of the 17th Amendment this would have been unnecessary.

If the responsibility of electing our U.S. Senators was returned to the State Legislatures, the cost of campaigns would be much lower. It obviously costs less to influence 150 Montana Legislators than it costs to influence the voters in a state of over 900,000 people. Rather than paying back the Legislatures in tax breaks, subsidies and lands to be exploited, the Federal Government would consider the will of the various state governments when making its laws. We would not have mandatory student testing being imposed upon us by the federal government.

WHY WON'T WE HAVE THE SAME PROBLEMS THAT BROUGHT US TO THE 17TH AMENDMENT

There were 2 main reasons the 17th Amendment was adopted in 1913.

One was the deadlock of State Legislatures when electing U.S. Senators. According to the Montana Historical Society Legislative Minute for January 15:

On this day in Montana legislative history January 15, 1890 the state's First Legislative Assembly already had been deadlocked for 54 days and there was no hope in sight of breaking the stalemate. In the House, 25 Republicans faced 25 Democrats. Here, however, a crucial 5 seats were disputed because of apparent voting irregularities in Silver Bow County's Precinct 34, at Homestake Tunnel above Butte. Both parties claimed the 5 swing seats and, thus, control of the House. Control was especially important because, prior to 1912, Montana legislators elected the state's U.S. Senators. So, to protect their 5 disputed seats, each party met in separate chambers for the duration of the 90 day session. In effect, two houses of representatives existed each one calling the other the rump house.

Regarding the most crucial question, Republican legislators elected two of their own as U.S. Senators Wilber Fisk Sanders and Thomas C. Power. And Democrats sent two of their own William A. Clark and Martin Maginnis to Washington. Since Republicans controlled Congress, Sanders and Power became Montana's first U.S. Senators.

The other was the corruption of the State Legislators. In Montana W.A. Clark bribed our state legislators in order to become a U.S. Senator.

In January 1889 it was reported that W.A. Clark;s son promised: We will send the old man to the Senate or the poorhouse. On January 10, 1889 a joint legislative committee to investigate reports of bribery presented sworn testimony to the legislature. The key testimony was that of State Senator Fred Whiteside of Flathead County. Whiteside testified that Clark's henchmen, led by attorney John B. Wellcome, had given him thirty thousand dollars to purchase his vote and the votes of several other legislators. He said that his exposure of Clark's bribe had brought threats to his life, but if this be the last act of my life, it is well worth the price to the people of this state.

WHAT IS OUR PROTECTION TODAY?

Our protection from corrupt State Legislatures are: Term limits; Campaign disclosure statements; Open Caucuses; and We have highly visible public information.

Our protection from dead-locked State Legislatures is the provision that if a State Legislature does not fill a vacancy or elect a U.S. Senator within 30 days, the Governor shall appoint the U.S. Senator.

I recommend that committee members give extra careful consideration to this proposal. This vote has historic and fundamental ramifications that go back to our founding fathers. We should not be impeded from following the patriotism and wisdom of our Constitution's framers.

Regarding opponents of the measure as Shakespeare said, they are thinking to precisely on the event and are 1 part wise, but 3 parts fearful.

THE FOUNDING FATHERS' SUCCESS FORMULA

The first volume of Sir Edmund Gibbons' lengthy 27-volume thesis entitled "The Rise and Fall of the Roman Empire" was released to the public in 1776. This exhaustive work detailed both the principles that build empires, and the principles that sow the seeds of destruction of empires. The Founding Fathers capitalizing on this and hundreds of additional historical and political works crafted one of the greatest works ever to come from the pen of mankind--the Constitution of the United States of America. Balancing the nature of mortal men against other mortal men's desires for power, this Constitution set the three branches of government to serve as watchdogs against each others encroachment of power, and States governments watching the Federal government.

Central in this complex formula was the United States Senate. In the Senate, the crossroads of power, rested the safeguard against future King George-like-bureaucrats. However, in 1913 a change in the Founding Fathers' success formula was orchestrated that completely changed the face of our governmental checks and balances.

We are all familiar with the horizontal separation of powers, which divided the power to govern into three branches, the executive, the legislative, and the judicial, leaving no one department of government with enough power to abuse the people. Remember, the abuses and oppressions of King George were fresh on their minds. Sovereignty was the battle cry.

However, today few know that the Founders also divided that same power vertically between the Federal Government and the State Governments. How would you protect the state governments?

James Madison, in discussing protection of the state governments from encroachment by the national government, suggested that they make the states part of the Federal Government!

The Founders did it by granting each state, large or small, two representatives in the Federal Government. These representatives were called Senators. They were chosen by the legislature of each state. They answered only to that states' legislature! This placed them above the influence of special interest groups, the media, and, to a great extent, political party bias, since members of all political parties in the state legislature chose them. The state's representatives were given power to veto or monitor all three branches of the federal government!!

After all, each piece of legislation, all judicial appointees, and all Executive appointments had to be approved by the Senate. As for national and foreign issues, all treaties, and all military affairs had to have the Senate's approval. Thus the states had a hand in all Federal affairs and each state's sovereignty was protected. In this manner the legislator you elected from your neighborhood had a direct influence in all federal affairs and could be held accountable by you, his neighbor.

Hence, the Constitution dictated that the Senators were to be chosen by the state legislatures and the federal government was granted only a limited number of powers. Only powers requiring cooperation of all the states-- national defense, foreign affairs, and interstate commerce. The remainder of powers was given to the states and/or held in reserve by the people.

Because of the Founders concern over the central governments ability to abuse the people, and because the states were closer to the citizens of each state and thus they could more readily be held accountable by the people, the Founders gave the states the responsibility of directly governing the people.

This all-important vertical separation of powers, dividing the power to govern vertically between the States and the Federal Government, was lost with the passage of the I7th Amendment

Since the passing of the 17th Amendment in 1913, the Federal Government has exploded out of control, usurping the rightful power of State Governments to govern the people. As the power was wrested from state elected officials, it was transferred to non-elected Federal officials who do not answer to the people because the people do not vote them in nor out of office. Thus any government official not directly reporting to a specific elected official is out of the control of the people. From these officials there is no redress!

We need to return to the Founding Fathers Success Formula, which kept government leaders "chained down by the Constitution" and accountable to the people. We can do this by repealing the 17th Amendment.

Returning the various powers to govern from Washington D. C. to the states would automatically bring about campaign finance reform. Senators would not be pressured to solicit money from any special interest group nor deal with media phobia, nor the prejudice of spur of the moment opinion polls.

These are times of change; most recently some of the changes are monumental. While we would rather ignore some of the consequences of these changes– some we just cannot ignore. For example many historical scholars are finding some alarming comparisons in today's events with some of the mistakes of the past. Are the "seeds of destruction that crumbled ancient Rome" as outlined by Gibbons, evident in our civilization in our day?

Some find change too challenging to contend with, while others invite the opportunity to make a difference. If you see a need, or feel a desire, to serve your country, perhaps Friends For America has some answers.

Friends For America-- a non-profit Corp.–was founded by volunteers to bring about a rebirth of freedom by restoring the balance of powers between the state governments and national government. Educating state legislators of their responsibility to maintain states rights and sovereignty is our mission. We have met with great success in our meetings with numerous state legislators, and are now in the process of setting up chapters in each state across the nation. We continue to find great support from local ranchers, businessmen, and trade associations. As we organize chapters in your area, city, or state, your individual efforts can have great effect!

PROCEDURE TO RESCIND THE 17TH AMENDMENT
TENTH AMENDMENT

On accepting the Constitution, people of the States' Governments forced the Framers of the Constitution to come up with the ten amendments that are chiseled in stone named the Bill of Rights to defend their rights.

The possibility of a corrupted Federal Government, encouraged the Framers of the Constitution to created the Tenth Amendment allowing the states to rescind Federal Government Amendments.

Article V of the Constitution sets forth the procedure for adding new amendments. Do you think that two thirds of the United States Senate would repeal themselves? Of course not!

The Framers of the Constitution recognized the power of the States' Governments and their citizens over the Federal Government. The 10th Amendment of the Constitution declares that "the powers not delegated to the United States by the Constitution, nor prohibited by it to the States, are reserved to the States respectively, or to the people."

The 10th Amendment places the authority to rescind Federal Government Amendments in the hands of the members of the States Governments' Legislatures whom represent the States Governments' people. The Constitution declares that the States Governments' people delegate those powers that the Federal Government may exercise. It takes three fourths of the States' Governments to remove or rescind an amendment.

Article V of the Constitution provides the requirements for adding new amendments to the Constitution but remains silent pertaining to removing or rescinding existing amendments; and by the supreme power retained by the 10th Amendment the states reserve the power to act whenever the Constitution remains silent and hereby call for the rescission of the 17th Amendment.

RESOLUTION TO RESCIND THE 17TH AMENDMENT

A RESOLUTION OF THE SOVEREIGN STATE OF _____ DECLARING AS DEFECTIVE THE CURRENT PROCESS OF SELECTING UNITED STATES SENATORS, PETITIONING CONGRESS THAT SAID STATE HEREBY GIVES NOTICE IT CHOOSES TO RESCIND THE 17TH AMENDMENT OF THE CONSTITUTION OF THE UNITED STATES AND RETURN TO THE PROCESSES PROMULGATED UNDER ARTICLE I, SECTION 3, CLAUSE 1 OF THE CONSTITUTION WHICH SET FORTH THAT UNITED STATES SENATORS SHALL BE CHOSEN BY THE STATE LEGISLATURE AND CLAUSE 2 WHICH PRESCRIBES THE METHOD OF FILLING VACANCIES AND OTHER PROCEDURES. THIS SOLEMN RESOLUTION HAS BEEN CONSIDERED DULY AND CONSUMMATED FOR THE REASONS AS FOLLOW:

WHEREAS, the Founding Fathers came to a great compromise at the Constitutional Convention of 1787 and provided for proportional representation in the House of Representatives of the United States and equal representation for the states in the Senate of the United States; and

WHEREAS, the Founding Fathers determined that equal representation of the states in the Senate of the United States recognized the individual sovereignty of each state; and

WHEREAS, Alexander Hamilton in the Federalist Papers, Number 27, concluded that because the legislatures were "select bodies of men", the choice of United States Senators would generally be made "with peculiar care and judgment" by the legislatures, a selection process originally provided for in Article I, Section 3, Clause 1, of the Constitution of the United States; and

WHEREAS, In Article IV, Section 4 of the Constitution "The United States shall guarantee to every State in this Union a republican form of government," yet the operation of the 17th Amendment supplanted the republic of the United States and republican form of government with a democracy, which was not the intent of the framers of the Constitution; and

WHEREAS, the 10th amendment declared a division of authority between the states and the United States and was for the first 140 years of this nation invoked by the Supreme Court of the United States as a constitutional limit of congressional power as against the powers of the several states; and

WHEREAS, the election of United States Senators by the State Legislatures was the political mechanism against congressional encroachments into the sovereignties of the states; and

WHEREAS, one of the essential aspects of the states' exercise of this political mechanism is the United States Senate's advice and consent for treaties and appointments of executive and judicial officers made by the President of the United States; and

WHEREAS, the ratification of the 17th Amendment in 1913 changed the election of the United States Senators from the State Legislatures to the popular vote of the people of the states, thereby divesting the states of any direct voice in the federal government; and

WHEREAS, Alexander Hamilton in Federalist Papers, Number 9, elaborating on the suffrages of the states in the Senate, said: "The proposed Constitution, so far from implying an abolition of the State governments, makes them constituent parts of the national sovereignty, by allowing them a direct representation in the Senate, and leaves in their possession certain exclusive and very important portions of sovereign power (underline added)."; and

WHEREAS, there can be no "states' rights" as a result of the 17th Amendment; and

WHEREAS, because of the differing modes of representation and election in the House and the Senate prior to 1913, each branch provided a balance of legislative power against, and an independent check upon, the other; and

WHEREAS, prior to 1913, history reveals that in choosing their Senators, the individual State Legislatures supported the federal government, thereby providing harmony between the governments of the states and the government of the United States; and

WHEREAS, the Congress of the United States has, since the ratification of the 17th Amendment, steadily encroached upon the sovereignty of this and the other states united by and under the Constitution of the United States; and

WHEREAS, a Senator's general responsibility is to represent state government and the State Legislature; and

WHEREAS, the State Legislature has a role in compelling accountability from United States Senators; and

WHEREAS, a state has the power to prescribe its own procedures regarding the selection process for United States Senators, including appointments in the case of deadlock; and

WHEREAS, Article V of the Constitution provides in pertinent part that " ...no State, without its consent, shall be deprived of its ... suffrage in the Senate", declaring that no amendment can deny the states of their suffrages in the United States Senate unless all the states consent, and the legislatures of several states withheld their ratifications of the 17th Amendment rendering defective any requirement making it mandatory that United States Senators shall be "elected by the people thereof" as prescribed by the 17th Amendment; and the 17th Amendment may have created an alternative method of selecting United States Senators - either appointment by the Legislature or election by popular vote of the people - whereas each state consents to the method of selection; and

WHEREAS, the 17th Amendment does not repeal or amend, express or implied, Article V of the Constitution; and

WHEREAS, the 17th Amendment does not repeal Article I, Section 3, Clause 1 of the Constitution which declares in pertinent part that two United States Senators from each state shall be "chosen by the Legislature thereof"; and

WHEREAS, the 17th Amendment cannot supersede Article I, Section 3, Clause 1 of the Constitution which specifies in pertinent part that two United States Senators from each state shall be "chosen by the Legislature thereof", since the 17th Amendment was not ratified by all the states and therefore did not receive the consents of all the states, and any amendment which deprives any state of its suffrage without its consent in the United States Senate is precluded by Article V of the Constitution; and

WHEREAS, the 17th Amendment failed to obtain ratifications in three-fourths of the states required by Article V of the Constitution as evidenced by Public Law 204 (August 7, 1953); and

WHEREAS, Article V of the Constitution provides the requirements for adding new amendments to the Constitution but remains silent pertaining to removing or rescinding existing amendments; and by the supreme power retained by the 10th Amendment the states reserve the power to act whenever the Constitution remains silent and hereby call for the rescission of the 17th Amendment.

STATES GOVERNMENTS' LEGISLATURES MUST RESCIND THE 17TH AMENDMENT

Although the Governor is the leader of the State Government, the Framers of the Constitution gave the States Governments' legislatures the most important job in the State Government. The States Government' legislatures whom are in closer communication with the States' constituencies than any other Federal Government faction like the United States House of Representatives are given the authority to pick the two United States Senators (ambassadors) for the Federal Government in order to return to a Republic form of Government.

The members of the State's legislature must not shirk from performing the mission assigned to them. Like soldiers in the field of battle, the legislatures must fight to return the government of the United States from a Democratic form of Government to a Republic form of Government that will guarantee sovereignty to the Federal Government as well as to the States' Governments resulting in protecting the rights of the people at large.

The Framers of the Constitution visualized the importance of balance of power to maintain a Republic form of Government within the Sovereign boundaries of the United States territory. That balance of power has eroded in favor of the Federal Government being influenced through the efforts of special interest groups whose only aim is to control the Federal Government, itself.

The Framers of the Constitution knew of special interest groups when the Constitution was being formed and finally written.

Today, the same States Governments' voters elect States' Governors and a United States Senator; therefore, in reality, the United States Senator title should be changed to Federal Governor. In every State of the union there exist a two to one (2/1) advantage of Federal Governors over a State Governor (due to the 17th Amendment). Over the entire nation there exist one hundred (100) Federal Governors against fifty (50) State Governors. Federal Governors and States' Governors are all independent entities ruling over the same people. Both Federal Governors and States' Governors have dictatorial powers. But, however, the States' Governors must answer to the States Governments' Legislatures whom are closely in communication with the inhabitants of the States Governments through the States' Senates and States' Assemblies reducing the States' Governors from being dictators to legislative type States' Governors. Not so with the Federal Governors whom answer to no one within the States. But, in the nation, the Federal Governors only answers to House Representatives. In all territorial States, the Federal Governors maintain dictatorial powers passing legislation against the will of the territorial States Governments' inhabitance whom have lost their rights (due to the 17th Amendment) to participate through the States Governments' Legislatures.

In the United States there are 1971 State Senate Districts 5411 State Assembly Districts. Add both and there are 7,382 States Governments' districts in the nation whereas there are only 435 House of Representative districts. Who is incommunicado with people of the nation? Of course, the answer is the States' Governments! The Framers of the Constitution knew this. The maintaining of power between the States' Governments and the Federal Government within a Republic form of Government belongs to the States' Governments and their inhabitance through the States Governments' legislatures not to the Federal Government.

SUMMARY

It behooves the States Governments' Legislatures must implement the Tenth Amendment to rescind the 17th Amendment in order to bring back a Republic form of Government to the United States of America and restore the rights of the people so that the people can take part in a wholesome Federal Government.

Remember, members of the Legislatures are people as is mentioned in this presentation!

Members of 7,382 States Governments' (State Senate and State Assembly) districts and 435 House of Representative districts have lost their Federal Governments' rights under the 17th Amendment; moreover, instead of dealing with 6,852 members of States Governments' Legislatures and 435 House of Representatives' members, the President negotiates with 435 House of Representatives' members and 100 United States Senates' members under the 17th Amendment.

Disenfranchisement of the States Governments' Legislatures and inhabitances is obvious here.

The importance of the States Governments' Legislatures lies in the fact that the Framers of the Constitution gave the States Governments' Legislatures the power to pick United States senators whom will act as ambassadors.

A good reason for the Framers of the Constitution to have the members of the United States Senate be ambassadors representatives of States' Governments is that the United States Senate is the most important active legislative body in the Federal Government.

Keep in mind that the States' Governments of the past created the Federal Government to form a Republic form of Government through the written Constitution.

Do not avoid responsibility! Bringing together States' Governments and Federal Government is the job of the States Governments' legislatures.

APPENDIX A

VOTER DISENFRANCHISEMENT
PRESIDENT'S TRIAD FRAMERS OF THE CONSTITUTION'S AMENDMENT (GOVERNOR EXCLUDED)

COMBINATIONS NUMBERS	PRESIDENT	US ASSEMBLY	STATE SENATOR	STATE ASSEMBLY
1	N	N	N	N
2	N	Y	N	N
3	N	N	N	N
4	N	N	Y	N
5	N	N	N	Y
6	N	Y	N	N
7	N	Y	Y	N
8	N	Y	N	Y
9	N	N	Y	N
10	N	N	N	Y
11	N	N	Y	Y
12	N	Y	Y	N
13	N	Y	N	Y
14	N	Y	Y	Y
15	N	N	Y	Y
16	N	Y	Y	Y
17	Y	N	N	N
18	Y	Y	N	N
19	Y	N	N	N
20	Y	N	Y	N
21	Y	N	N	Y
22	Y	Y	N	N
23	Y	Y	Y	N
24	Y	Y	N	Y
25	Y	N	Y	N
26	Y	N	N	Y
27	Y	N	Y	Y
28	Y	Y	Y	N
29	Y	Y	N	Y
30	Y	Y	Y	Y
31	Y	N	Y	Y
32	Y	Y	Y	Y

Table 1

PRESIDENT'S TRIAD FRAMERS OF THE CONSTITUTION'S AMENDMENT
(PRESIDENT AND GOVERNOR EXCLUDED)

COMBINATIONS NUMBERS	US ASSEMBLY	STATE SENATOR	STATE ASSEMBLY
1	N	N	N
2	N	N	N
3	N	Y	N
4	N	N	Y
5	N	Y	N
6	N	N	Y
7	N	Y	Y
8	Y	Y	Y
9	Y	N	N
10	Y	N	N
11	Y	Y	N
12	Y	N	Y
13	Y	Y	N
14	Y	N	Y
15	Y	Y	Y
16	Y	Y	Y

Table 2

PRESIDENT'S TRIAD 17 AMENDMENT

COMBINATIONS NUMBERS	PRESIDENT	SENATE OR FEDERAL GOVERNOR	US ASSEMBLY
1	N	N	N
2	N	Y	N
3	N	N	Y
4	N	Y	Y
5	Y	N	N
6	Y	Y	N
7	Y	N	Y
8	Y	Y	Y

Table 3

PRESIDENT'S TRIAD 17 AMENDMENT PRESIDENT EXCLUDED

COMBINATIONS NUMBERS	SENATE OR FEDERAL GOVERNOR	US ASSEMBLY
1	N	N
2	Y	N
3	N	Y
4	Y	Y

Table 4

PICK SENATOR OR AMBASSADOR FRAMERS OF THE CONSTITUTION'S AMENDMENT

COMBINATIONS NUMBERS	STATE SENATOR	STATE ASSEMBLY
1	N	N
2	Y	N
3	N	Y
4	Y	Y

Table 5

PICK SENATOR OR FEDERAL GOVERNOR 17 AMENDMENT

COMBINATIONS NUMBERS	SENATE OR FEDERAL GOVERNOR
1	N
2	Y

Table 6

http://www.claremont.org/publications/crb/id.1155/article_detail.asp
http://www.liberty-ca.org/friendsforamerica.org.htm
http://liberty-ca.org/seventeenth_amendment.htm
http://www.articlev.com/repeal17.htm
http://www.articlev.com/repeal_the_17th_amendment.htm
http://repealthe17thamendment.blogspot.com/
http://repealthe17thamendment.blogspot.com/2007/02/utah-senate-bill-b202.html
http://www.nationalreview.com/nrof_bartlett/bartlett200405120748.asp
http://archives.cnn.com/2002/LAW/09/17/fl.dean.17th.amendment/
http://en.wikipedia.org/wiki/Seventeenth_Amendment_to_the_United_States_Constitution#Criticism
http://www.liberty-ca.org/articles/macmullin_17th.htm
http://www.whynot.net/ideas/1249
http://www.jeffryfisher.net/Statesman/ElectionLaw/Repeal17.htm
http://www.liberty-ca.org/repeal17/states/montana2003oneil.htm
http://writ.corporate.findlaw.com/dean/20020913.html
http://www.lewrockwell.com/orig/tucker7.html
http://www.mises.org/article.aspx?Id=545
http://www.sovereigncause.org/strategy.html#page2
http://sovereigncause.org/template.html
http://liberty-ca.org/presentations/articles/ampliffying10th/amp10_01.htm
http://www.constitution.org/fed/federa10.htm
http://www.constitution.org/fed/federa51.htm
http://www.yale.edu/lawweb/avalon/federal/fed27.htm
http://www.mises.org/article.aspx?Id=545
http://www.mises.org/article.aspx?Id=533
http://www.freerepublic.com/focus/f-bloggers/1972454/posts
http://www.freerepublic.com/focus/f-news/1937187/posts
http://www.freerepublic.com/focus/f-bloggers/1936817/posts

www.ingramcontent.com/pod-product-compliance
Lightning Source LLC
Chambersburg PA
CBHW052008280526
45793CB00005B/895